CERAMIC VARIABILITY

CERAMIC VARIABILITY

An Ethnographic Perspective

SHARMI CHAKRABORTY

PRIMUS BOOKS

PRIMUS BOOKS

An imprint of Ratna Sagar P. Ltd.
Virat Bhavan
Mukherjee Nagar Commercial Complex
Delhi 110 009

Offices at
CHENNAI LUCKNOW
AGRA AHMEDABAD BENGALURU COIMBATORE DEHRADUN
GUWAHATI HYDERABAD JAIPUR JALANDHAR KANPUR KOCHI
KOLKATA MADURAI MUMBAI PATNA RANCHI VARANASI

First published 2018

ISBN: 978-93-86552-77-8 (hardback)
ISBN: 978-93-86552-78-5 (POD)

Published by Primus Books

Lasertypeset by Shine Graphics
Amar Colony, East Gokalpur, Delhi 110 094

Printed and bound in India by Replika Press Pvt. Ltd.

Contents

Tables

Figures and Map

FIGURES

MAP

Plates

Acknowledgements

THIS STUDY WAS supported by Centre for Archaeological Studies and Training, Eastern India (an autonomous institution of the Government of West Bengal). I am thankful to Professor Gautam Sengupta (former Member Secretary, CASTEI) and Smt. Sunrita Hazra (former Member Secretary, CASTEI) for their support. I have benefited from comments of Dr Anup Mishra, Dr Bisnnupriya Basak and Dr Sheena Panja. Dr V. Selvakumar had kindly gone through the manuscript in the initial stages and cleared many knots. I thank Professor Shereen Ratnagar for a thorough editing and making the research friendly to the readers. The base map used in the book is made by Sutapa Roy. A lot of my work in South 24 Parganas has been facilitated by Debisankar Middhya, without his enthusiastic support my task would have been very difficult. During my survey in the villages I received help from many like Srimati Pal of Kashinagar, Amar Pal of Raydighi Kachharibari, Shankar Pal of Tantirhat, Manik Pal of Nastika, Naru Pal of Ulkunda, Khudiram Pal Mahula, Sukumar Pal of Shyamnona, Dwipali Pal of Shudpur, Gopinath Pal of Ichchhabat, Kalipada Pal of Gafulia, Bhadreswari Pal of Krishnapalli, Haran Pal of Rabindrapalli, Panchanan Pal of Phulbaria, Arun Pal of Mathurapur, Dwipali Pal of Mohadipur, Badal Pal of Bishaypur, Pabitri Pal and Bhagyadhar Pal of Bonpara and others. Finally this book would not have been possible without support and encouragement of family and friends.

1

Introduction

THIS BOOK DEALS with pottery that is almost always so plentiful at archaeological sites. Containers and cooking vessels of earthenware are fragile and break easily as well as frequently. They can be easily replaced, however, as local clays and pre-industrial fuels and kilns, the resources for pottery production, were easily available. And then, earthenware unlike metal does not disintegrate when buried for centuries in a mound. Thus, pottery constitutes the major category of artefacts excavated at most sites.

We use the attributes—fabric, size, surface treatment, shape, nature of firing, etc.—of excavated pottery to distinguish various pottery assemblages from one another. A change in forms and fabric over time may indicate new usage and varying technologies. Thus, it is the details, the variables of ceramic assemblages, on which archaeological analysis focuses and ceramic variability has been a concern of archaeological investigations from the early years of the discipline. However, the terms and expressions, the questions asked, and the methods of investigation have all been varied. With new tools of documentation, a greater amount of variability is being exposed to the discerning eyes of researchers. This has made pottery analysis more fruitful and in many ways more complex.

My study aims to explore the variations that are created in ceramic assemblages in present-day production in order to understand the variations that are noticed archaeologically. It is restricted to those artefacts that are essentially containers, vessels used for long-term and short-term storage, and/or cooking purposes.

The study seeks to explore the reason for a particular paste on rim form or size of vessel in a known and restricted time frame and within a limited space, with the aim of evolving a conceptual framework for the reading of ceramic history. I am convinced that this would allow a better organization of observations and classification of attributes.

CERAMIC VARIABILITY

The subject of ceramic variability has been addressed by archaeologists time and again. It has also been used in discussions of style. Ceramic variations are classified according to certain specific attributes. An attribute reveals customary ways of manufacturing or using an artefact. Such conditions exclude the idiosyncrasies of individual potters or particular physical or chemical features of the raw material, or non-cultural features (Rouse 1960). In the type-variable system, a type is regarded as a set of fundamental attributes (Grifford 1960). Within a type, varieties are differentiated by minor characteristics produced by families or by individual potters. Here variety does not represent a cultural configuration. In India, the classification of ceramics is based on 'ware', which usually depends on fabric and is considered to have cultural implications. This is followed by separation into formal type within wares. This system evolved out of a need to catalogue finds.

The ultimate aims of all these operations mentioned above are to answer archaeological questions which are changing and evolving with time and various schools of thought. The empiricists tried to understand chronology with ceramic variability. Flinders Petrie (1904) commented on variations that are noticed in pottery with time, and reconstructed the chronology of the Neolithic pottery of Egypt (1920) on this basis.

The culture historical interpretation advocated observations of variability as evidence of migration and diffusion (Childe 1957, 1964). For the processualists the question was about the processes that bring about variation (Binford 1962). Binford (1965) divided formal variability into two broad classes with regard to socio-cultural context. '*Primary functional variation* is related to specific use made of the vessel in question.... *Secondary functional variation* is a by-product of social context of manufactures of the vessel or of the social context of intended use of the item or both.' According to Plogg (1980), spatial nature of stylistic variation is caused by adaptive strategy within a region by prehistoric groups which determine deposition of the artefacts, the relation between vessel shape and decoration, and its use and exchange of materials among prehistoric community. For behaviourists it is an expression of choices (Schiffer and Skibo 1997), from the collection of clay to the preparation of paste and the production of the pot to its marketing. Ceramic variability is also a product dictated by the *chaîne opéretoire* (Roux and Corbetta 1989) where the operational process including technical gestures interacts with the material world. For post-processualists, in contrast, variation symbolizes a gamut of thought and activity. It also includes the dialectic relationship between event and its interpretation (Hodder 1990).

While chronology is a continuing area of interest for archaeologists with different theoretical affiliations, inferences about complex issues like the migration of population and cultural diffusion is usually not restricted to ceramic variability any longer. The post-1960s theoretical perspectives are the results of archaeologists' widening horizon of interest and a need for a fuller understanding past behaviour and activity. Demography, gender, society, economy, polity, symbolic systems, exchange and ecology—the questions are many. This has led to a variety of research designs. This versatile implication of variability, as expressed through style, has been eloquently penned by Hodder (1990), 'Style is involved in social strategies of creating relationships and ideologies by fixing meaning according to established criterion. It includes the power to control special structures and the movement of people within them and it includes the ability to halt time or control its passing.'

In this work the term 'variation' has been preferred over 'style'. There are archaeologists who prefer to classify object attributes according to function and style (Dunnell 1978). However, another stream of thought considers style as expression of the identity, of an object, a person or a group (Sackett 1977; Hodder 1982, 1990; Conkey 1990). Style may be actively displayed in a manner Wiessner (1983) terms as 'emblematic', distinguishing one community from another. Over a period of time it may become simply a usage. The term variation involves all these aspects related to specific use, collective expression of a community, specific way of expression of an artisan or a particular aspect of a single pot.

The term 'variation' is often used in a loose way. It includes the unintentional differences that one may expect to be present in craft products.

This study is an attempt at understanding the variations in archaeological pottery. These largely fragmented artefacts are recorded according to their colour/firing, paste, proposed functional affiliation, and form. In complex societies there would be a wide range of entities under these variables. It is usual to arrange them in manageable groups suitable to address specific research questions. However, suitability depends on some prior understanding of, or hypothesis about, the character of the data. The success of classification and the following analysis will depend on that.

I deal with the concept of two variables mentioned above—functional affiliation and form. They are not mutually exclusive but in combination can be extremely diverse. Functions of archaeological pots are derived from their morphometry and with certain other formal qualities. These often serve as the categories by which groups are formed. There can be further subdivisions, according to variety of forms, that could be present within a functional category. In brief, the study of variability here is restricted to the shape and size of the ceramics. This includes human intentions, conscious and unconscious, as well as 'errors' in production.

ETHNOGRAPHY AND ETHNOARCHAEOLOGY

Middle Range Theory was initiated by 'processual' archaeologists for understanding the dynamic past from its static archaeological record. Ethnoarchaeology, in the broadest sense, the study of present to understand archaeological data, has been widely used but there is an ongoing debate whether ethnoarchaeology should fall under Middle Range Theory (Arnold 2003). There is also a debate regarding how many of the research projects carried out under the umbrella of ethnoarchaeology actually constitute ethnoarchaeology, and how many should fall simply under ethnography or material culture study (David and Kramer 2001). There has also been a debate whether ethnographic study can be relevant universally (Hodder 1986). With all its problems ethnography has become acceptable in archaeological circles irrespective of their theoretical leaning, as a viable tool for mediating with the past because without analogy it would be difficult to even call a pot 'a pot'. However, the need to design research and address problems related to ethnographic evidence should not be understated. The value of ethnographic inference and analogy is dependent on these issues, as we shall see.

In India, ethnographic data has been used to explain archaelogical phenomenon early in twentieth century by Marshall (1904–5) and Bhandarkar (1920) who have used their experience of the local use of ceramic forms to interpret archaelogical data. Post-Independence (1947), a survey was carried out under the direction of N.K. Bose (1947) on peasant life in India. Pottery making tradition(s) was also documented and published (Saraswati and Behura 1966). In the forward note Bose reflected that it could be of use to archaeologists and it has been proved to be so by the number of works which have referred to this volume since its publication.

In the Indian context ethnoarchaeological work to understand variability has been undertaken by Daniel Miller in Madhya Pradesh (1985) and Carol Kramer in Rajasthan (1997). The study of Carol Kramer is based on two urban centres of Rajasthan, where diverse earthen pots were produced and widely used. Her objective was to collect data about the diversity of pottery in modern settlements of different size, and to view the relation between urban and non-urban communities.

Miller based his work on a single village in Madhya Pradesh in an intensive study of how variability is produced by the human catagorization process. It involved study of rim types, form, body angularity—the very details that are studied in ancient pots to see what kind of information can be garnered from them. He feels that these variations are best understood in the context of their production, distribution and use. The study raises questions regarding specific variability in terms of social relations and how to approach this question through a study of objects as categories.

The aim of both these studies was to form a general theory that could be universally applicable. My research does not, however, aim at any universal model. It is grounded in the understanding of ceramic production in the Indian context.

Variations in form and decoration and their implications for classification have been discussed by Archana Choski (1995) based on a survey of two villages in Kutch. She tested the method of classification based on formal variation commonly used by archaeologists. It was found that in one village people classify their pottery according to decoration and function, while the other villagers classify them according to the caste which would use them.

Renu Bala's work (1997) draws attention to the size of container vessels in urban and rural society of the present in relation to archaeological pots, as she wishes to explore, much like Kramer, the urban and rural divide.

Sonia Bhagat (2001) made a comparison of the variation in size of Harappan pottery at Padri and present-day pottery of Tarasara village in Bhavnagar district in Gujarat. She noticed that potters of Tarasara village distinguish vessels on their overall shape, size, particular rim shapes, carination on the shoulder, slip and painting. She also noticed differences between the two potters making the same vessel in same vessel type, manufactured by two potters and variations in the type and in a single workshop.

Recently V. Vinod and K. Krishnan (2011) have discussed the notion of specialization and standardization, asking if specialization leads to standardization. Their study, based on Rice's (1981) work on coefficient of variance, explores the output of part-time as well as full-time potters of Gujarat. Here I restrict myself to full-time specialized potters and standardization of production which is conceptualized not only at the level of size but also of form and not only at the level of individual but also at the level of community.

PROBLEMS AND AIMS OF THIS RESEARCH

This work engages with ceramic variability through ethnography from a modified theoretical perspective. It takes into consideration ecology, historical process of the region concerned, and the operational sequence: these together generate variations. The scope of this work is wide, covering twenty-seven villages in West Bengal with physiographic differences within the same (Bengali) language. The emphasis is on cultural context—how village potters in a region of apparently homogenous culture, express differences in their output. It is an effort to discern strands of cultural matrix that contribute towards these variations.

At primary level it is about how classification is done according to shapes. The forms of pottery are named according to the function as perceived by the archaeologist. This is based on everyday experience. In India, it is a popular hypothesis among archaeologists that present shapes and functions of pottery are very similar to the archaeological counterparts. The terminology used for ceramic forms in archaeological literature, say *lota* or *handi*, therefore, carries this impression. Attempts have been made to base classification on morphometry of the shapes, such as that of Dales and Kenoyer (1986) whose work relates morphometry to function and shapes, which is easier to apply for classification purposes but can impose an unnecessary rigidity among classes.

At another level, the work focuses on a basic problem of the archaeological record: it rarely yields intact shapes. Documentation and detailed description, therefore, mostly involve the rim and the base. This has resulted in a variety of descriptions. Many of which, even if accurate, may be checked for over-description.

Ethnographic survey was undertaken keeping in mind the specific problems of archaeological interpretation.

- how much variation can be expected in pottery shape within groups inhabiting different regions and within groups of the same region,
- how do shapes for the same function can vary,
- how much variation can be expected within classes of pots manufactured by the same potter,
- what kind of change in manufacturing strategy the potter has to initiate in order bring about variation, and
- the cause of change and difference.

METHOD

Pottery production by pre-industrial methods has had a long history and has been extensively practised. Yet, social conditions have changed vastly over the last century and especially over the last thirty years. Inroads of urban lifestyles into villages have diminished the use of pottery. As a result, the number of potters and the number of types produced have fallen. Also there has been an introduction of new forms and innovations to keep enterprises safe from the onslaught of non-ceramic industrial products, which are more durable.

The studied region is restricted to the state of West Bengal. To understand inter and intraregional variability, three zones were selected—Malda region in the north, Birbhum-Bardhaman region in the west and South 24 Parganas in the south (see Chapter 2). These regions are located some distance apart from each other (Map 1.1) and are geographically different. The villages were selected on the basis of presence of a sizeable potter community making primarily storage/cooking vessels and at least a few shapes.

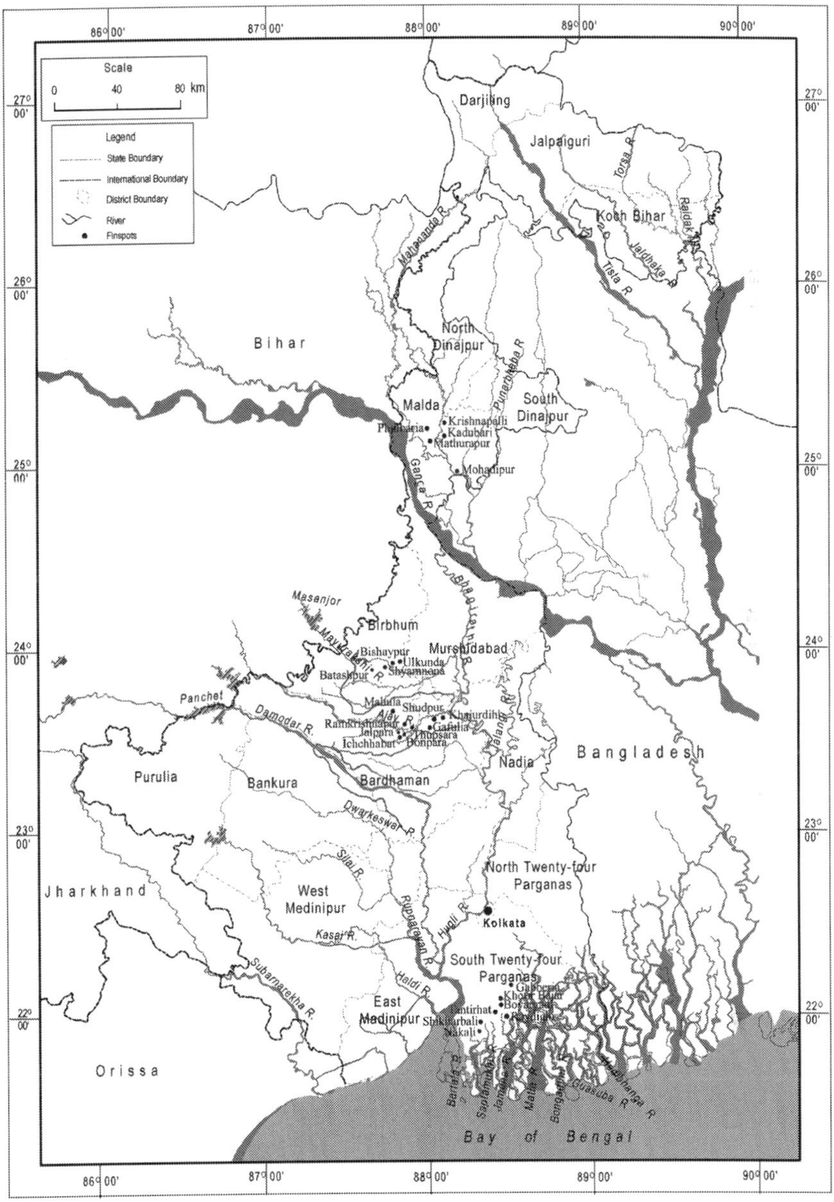

MAP 1.1: Surveyed villages of West Bengal

Ceramics of different sizes and shapes were recorded in each selected village from the house-cum-workshop of a few potters or from a single potter. This is dependent on the kind of evidence available and cooperation of the potters. Potters tend to work on a particular type at a time. This means that all the different shapes of their repertoire may or may not be present in a single house at a given time. In many villages the work is organized in such a way that a common kiln is utilized by many families. The arrangement of pottery in a kiln is according to shape and it is usual to put similar shapes together during firing, unless there is an immediate demand to the contrary. It is usual to have more demand for a particular type at a particular time.

Measurements were taken of the available forms, depending on the cooperation of the respective household. The emphasis has been on the rims because it is rim that mostly gets recorded in archaeological reports.

The aim is to record only the approximate sizes. The method has also not emphasized specific counts of samples. The aim was to see general trend of forms and sizes.

There are some practical problems also. Since a number of villages in the chosen regions were covered, it was not possible to regulate the time of the visit. Therefore, in some homes there were many samples which could be measured, but some had only a few, and in a few households all the pots were put in a kiln and none could be measured. Some pots which could be measured, were unfired. These would shrink after firing though not to a great extent, and in any case it is difficult to move unfired pieces around.

Chapter 3 uses the data generated in this survey for understanding variations in morphometry through statistical analysis. It also studies formal variations in these pots recorded from different regions of West Bengal.

The second phase of the work involved looking at variability within a local market to see the kind of variations that are present in different shops, asking from where they get their products and their clients (Chapter 4). Samples were also bought, measured and broken and drawn to see the amount of variation within each category.

The third phase of the work involved documenting manufacturing process to see how the different shapes are manufactured (Chapter 5). While variations in shape were recorded in different regions, the differences in the process of manufacture of different shapes on the wheel were documented at just one workshop. It is understood that people of different regions do certain things differently or some variations could exist within potters of the same region. But that has been kept out of the purview of present work due to time constraints.

The concluding chapter discusses how shapes are related to functions, techniques of production, chance and conscious creation or what can be considered a regional or local style. It also tries to look into recent history to understand spatial manifestations of style. It then discusses variations and classification of these variation that lead to archaeological interpretation.

2

The Survey

VARIABILITY OF PRESENT-DAY ceramic production was sampled in Malda district in the north, Birbhum and Bardhaman districts in the west and South 24 Parganas in the south of West Bengal. The places chosen for survey are based on earlier work (Ghosh 2002) and information from Mr Debishankar Middhya of South 24 Parganas who is interested in local history and traditional crafts. Some additional villages were chosen on the basis of information received during the survey. Villages reported to produce different types of vessels were preferred. It is also a fact that not every village has potters and where they are present, they often constitute a few households. Potters produce more often for a large number of villages and distribution takes place through the local markets (*hat*). People living within the radius of 10–15 km. usually buy and sell their products in these markets.

The dimensions of each ceramic type are given in a tabular format. The dimensions include diameters of rim, neck, body, height (all measured in centimetres) and the angle between the base and the month of the pot. In a deeper vessel, therefore, the opening would be less even if the diameter is the same. In many cases only the diameter of the rim is given. In those cases the pot is either incomplete or has been placed to dry out on a stand, therefore all the measurements are not available. These vessels are all round bottomed and hence the bases of the pots have been left out of the table.

BIRBHUM DISTRICT

This district in the west consists of the eastern fringe of the Chotanagpur plateau, pediplain of colluvium, alluvium, and lateritic soil formed over degenerated rock (Majumdar 1975). The most important rivers are Darakeswar, Mayurakshi and Ajay, which are joined by numerous small rivulets. The slope of the land is from west to east and the rivers drain into the river Bhagirathi in the east. The older alluvium, probably Middle Pleistocene, is coarse and reddish in colour with calcareous and limonite concretions and covers most of the area. The younger alluvium is confined to narrow strips near river channels. The Mayurakshi River is perennial only downstream and gives out two distributaries, the Kana and the Manikarnika. Ajay River, which makes the southern border with Bardhaman district, is prone to flood but that rarely affects Birbhum district.

The villages covered are given below. The jurisdictions of the districts are divided under police stations which will be henceforth mentioned as PS. The figures given in the tables that follow are in centimetres. In the columns are given rim diameter, the hamowest diameter of the neck, body diameter, height and the angle between the base and the month of the pot.

Nastika (Mayureswar PS)

The clay is from Manikarnika River. It is not very fine. In it is then mixed some coarse sand of Mayurakshi, or else ash from the oven, to make the paste. Pottery here is mostly made in moulds, although some are partly formed on the wheel. The slip is made from the same clay. Chalk bought from the market is used for the white colour for decorations on the pots for rituals though there are natural sources of keolinite clay in the district. The treatment given to all pots is the same irrespective of their functions

TABLE 2.1: Ceramic types from Nastika

pot type	*rim (in cm.)*	*neck (in cm.)*	*body (in cm.)*	*height (in cm.)*	*opening (in cm.)*
date pitcher (see Pl. 4.3)	13	–	–	–	–
frying pan (see Pl. 3.9)	27.5	–	28.5	15	100
handi (see Pl. 3.3)	40	37	46.5	33	64
lid	11.5		11.6	1.1	110
muri roaster (see Pl. 3.5)	29.5	–	–	–	–
muri roaster	47.5	–	–	–	102
muri sieve (see Pl. 3.6)	30	–	32	16.5	78
malsa (see Pl. 3.12)	21.5	20	22	11.5	94
malsa	29	27.5	32.5	20	80
malsa	24.5	–	–	–	–
ghata (see Pl. 3.11)	15.5	13.3	21.5	18.5	60
ghata	13.5	11	20.5	20	40
patna (for feeding cattle)	40	–	–	–	–
patna (see Pl. 3.7)	44	–	–	–	–
patna	48	–	–	–	–
water pitcher (see Pl. 1.1)	14	9	23	25	26
water pitcher	16	12	25	25	40
water pitcher	13	9	23	25	26
chatu for *pithe* or *ruti* (see Pl. 3.8)	29.5	–	27	3	150

(except those for ritualistic purposes) (Table 2.1). Slip is applied on all kinds of pottery and is termed 'polish'. The market is at Kotasur, located nearby.

Bataspur (Mayureswar PS)

The market is again at Kotasur. The potters also sell in the weekly market at Mayureswar and locally from their homes/workshops. They collect clay from ponds, tank and the Manikarnika River. This is mixed with sand and ash of medium size. The pots are wheel-made, handmade and mould made (Table 2.2). The fuel for the kiln (*sal*) is straw and Palmyra palm leaves.

Other clay artefacts that are made include the oil press for sesame, a tube for smoking cannabis (*kolke*), the ritual horse, and a money pot.

Ulkunda (Kotasur PS)

Here too wheel-made, handmade and mould-made methods have been used for making pottery. In this village clay is collected from a sluice cut from the bank of the Mayurakshi River. It is mixed with clayey soil of the pond, sand from the Mayurakshi River and ash. The ash is not used to prepare the paste but is put on the mould and the body of the pot so

TABLE 2.2: Ceramic types from Bataspur

pot type	*rim (in cm.)*	*neck (in cm.)*	*body (in cm.)*	*height (in cm.)*	*opening (in cm.)*
pithe malsa (perforated)	19	–	–	–	–
pithe bowl	23	–	–	–	–
pithe bowl for muslim	30	–	–	–	–
kadai (frying pan)	29	–	–	–	–
kadai (frying pan)	23	–	–	–	–
handi	26	24	27.5	17.5	72
lid	12.5	–	–	–	–
muri roaster	55	–	–	–	–
muri roaster	52	–	–	–	–
muri sieve	30	–	–	–	–
paddy boiling pot	35.5	–	–	–	–
rice pot (see Pl. 3.4)	28	25	32	21.5	66
ghata	14	11.4	17.5	18.2	44
ghata	10	8.5	14	13.5	40
chatu	29	–	–	–	–
patna	40	–	–	–	–
patna	45	–	–	–	–
water jar	16.5	14.4	29	30	30
water jar	28	23	46	47	36

TABLE 2.3: Ceramic types from Ulkunda

pot type	*rim (in cm.)*
kadai (frying pan)	29
kadai (frying pan)	25
patna	52
patna	37
handi for cooking vegetables	23
chatu	29

that the clay does not stick to the surface of the dabber while it is used in beating the pot.

The colour for the slip is made out of red lateritic soil. It is bought from Kandi Bazar in Murshidabad district, located not very far from the village. The nodules are soaked, dried and made into paste.

The pots found in the village were in different stages of production. Therefore, the table above only gives the size of the rim (Table 2.3). The market is at Shat Paisar Gram and Ramnagar.

Mahula (Bolpur PS)

In this village the clay as well as the sand for the potters' workshops come from the Kopai River. The material for the slip, that is, red lateritic soil, comes from Palashdanga, some 15 km. away. The market is at Bolpur. Types of pots are given in Table 2.4.

Shyamnona (Bolpur PS)

The clay and sand come from Kopai and the raw material for slip comes from Palashdanga. The market is at Bolpur. Here too pots are made in moulds as well as on a wheel (Table 2.5).

Bishaypur (Labhpur PS)

In this village the potters collect the clay from the local pond. The sand comes from Mayurakshi. The material for the slip comes from Baltoli in Murshidabad district. Ash is used only to prevent the pottery from sticking to the mould. Here also both wheel-made and mould-made pottery are manufactured (Table 2.6).

Ramkrishnapur (Bolpur PS)

The clay comes from a local water body called Kanon Dighi. The sand comes from the Ajay River and colour for the slip comes from Domunia near

TABLE 2.4: Ceramic types from Mahula

pot type	*rim (in cm.)*	*neck (in cm.)*	*body (in cm.)*	*height (in cm.)*	*opening (in cm.)*
frying pan	30.5	–	–	12.8	100
muri roaster	64	–	54	21	110
muri siever	29	–	30.5	16	90
rice pot	29	25.6	32	20	80
rice pot	24	23	28	20.5	60
ritual bowl	30	–	31.5	20	82
ritual pot	6	5.5	7	7	52
ritual pot	4	3.5	4.5	4.5	50
vegetable pot (see Pl. 3.10)	26	–	–	–	–
water pitcher	14.5	10.5	32.6	29.5	26
patna	49	–	–	–	–

Ahmadpur which is more than 20 km. away from the village. Like the rest of the villages, here too pottery is mostly formed on the wheel and some are made in moulds but large jars are made by joining slabs (Table 2.7).

The market is at Bosepara, Natunhat and Bolpur. Other than these utensils, the potters also manufacture *baya* and *khol* (musical drums) and *unan* (portable stove).

Thupsara (Bolpur PS)

The clay is acquired by the potters from Kanon Dighi as in the previous case; the sand is from *kandor* (rivulet) near Bosepara and colour for slip is bought from Ahmadpur or Palashdanga. They also manufacture pottery stoves with a diameter of about 23.5 cm. The pots are either wheel-made or mould-made (Table 2.8).

TABLE 2.5: Ceramic types from Shyamnona

pot type	*rim (in cm.)*	*neck (in cm.)*	*body (in cm.)*	*height (in cm.)*	*opening (in cm.)*
alcohol making pot	16	13	23.5	22.4	44
date pitcher	16	–	–	–	–
kadai	29	–	30	25	106
lid	16.5	–	–	–	–
muri chalni (roaster)	63	–	–	–	–
muri chhaka (sieve)	30	–	–	–	–
rice pot	20	–	–	–	–
ritual pot	12	9.6	15	13.5	40
tawa	29	–	–	14.8	140
kalash (water pitcher)	16	13	30	30	30
kalash	19	–	37	43	30
water pot (see Pl. 3.2)	16	13	23	22.5	44

TABLE 2.6: Ceramic types from Bishaypur

pot type	*rim (in cm.)*	*neck (in cm.)*	*body (in cm.)*	*height (in cm.)*	*opening (in cm.)*
kadai (frying pan)	28	–	–	–	–
kadai (frying pan)	24	–	–	–	–
lid	23	–	21.5	5	140
lid	13	–	–	–	–
muri chalni	52	–	–	–	–
muri chalni	42	–	–	–	–
muri chhaka	29	–	–	–	–
paddy boiling pot	24	21.5	31.5	28	50
rice pot	24	21.5	31.5	28	50
ritual pot	13.5	–	–	–	–
vegetable pot	23	19	21	13	70
water jar	13	–	–	–	–

Satne (Bolpur PS)

The potters in Satne use the same sources and methods of production as the nearby village of Thupsara.

The potting community on the Ajay River has to acquire the clay for red slip from the lateritic soil area which is to the north. Outcrops are much closer to Mayurakshi than to Ajay.

TABLE 2.7: Ceramic types from Ramkrishnapur

pot type	*rim (in cm.)*	*neck (in cm.)*	*body (in cm.)*	*height (in cm.)*	*opening (in cm.)*
kadai	29	–	–	–	–
lid	10.5	–	10.6	3	130
muri chalni	68	–	–	–	–
muri chalni	58	–	–	–	–
muri chhaka	33	–	–	–	–
rice pot	20	19	33.5	29.5	40
rice pot	17.5	15	27	27.5	40
ritual pot	14.5	12	16.4	19.5	40
small pot	11	9	12.5	15	42
tawa	29	–	–	–	–
patna (basin)	37	–	–	–	–
patna (basin)	49.5	–	–	–	–
vegetable pot	30	–	–	–	–
vegetable pot	25	–	–	–	–
water pitcher	14.5	10.4	28	28	30

Table 2.8: Ceramic types from Thupsara

pot type	*rim (in cm.)*	*neck (in cm.)*	*body (in cm.)*	*height (in cm.)*	*opening (in cm.)*
tijel for Muslim (beef pot)	29.5	27.3	44.5	41.5	34
kadai (frying pan)	30	–	33.5	15	100
kadai (frying pan)	23.5	–	25	11	100
muri chalni (roaster)	61	–	–	–	–
muri chhaka (sieve)	30	–	33	13.5	94
paddy jar	19	16.5	42.5	50.5	20
tal handi (Palmyra juice pot)	18	15	25	22.5	48
rice pot	20	15.5	25	22	52
biyer bhar (marriage pot)	14.5	–	17.4	10	80
biyer bhar (marriage pot)	12	–	–	–	–
tawa	21	–	–	–	–
patna (basin)	56	–	46	42	80
vegetable pot	26	23.5	31	18	90
water jar	19	16.5	42.5	50.5	20

BARDHAMAN

The physiography of Bardhaman is similar to that of Birbhum except that the rivers are larger. Two most important rivers are Ajay and Damodar. In the context of this survey, the Ajay River is important and is known to flood. There are different kinds of soil in this region (Chaudhuri, et al. 1994). The red lateritic soil merges into alluvium in the east. The highest alluvial terrace is of older alluvium, mature, highly leached and moderately acidic. The next terrace is formed by mature moderately drained brownish sandy-to-clayey loam. The lowest terrace is within the limits of high floods and consists of sandy soil. The alluvial soil may be grouped into sand, sandy loam, silty loam, clayey loam and clay. These are well drained, acidic and poor in organic matter.

TABLE 2.9: Ceramic types from Satne

pot type	*rim (in cm.)*
tijel for Muslim (beef pot)	30
lid	23
muri chalni (roaster)	69
muri chalni	62
muri chalni	57
muri chhaka (sieve)	30
rice pot	20
ritual pot	14
tawa	29
vegetable pot	26

Bonpara Shimultala (Mangalkot PS)

This village has a large potter community of forty households. The soil comes from nearby pond, the sand from Natunhat. The material for the slip comes from Palashban or Damur near Rampurhat, which is quite far. The pottery is mostly manufactured on mould and by hand and sometimes on wheel (Table 2.10). The market is at Nigan and nearby villages.

TABLE 2.10: Ceramic types from Bonpara

pot type	*rim (in cm.)*	*neck (in cm.)*	*body (in cm.)*	*height (in cm.)*	*opening (in cm.)*
date juice pot	17	15	23.6	19.3	52
frying pan	20	–	27.5	12	110
frying pan	32	–	33	13.5	108
frying pan	30	–	28.5	13	108
handi	23	–	28.1	17.8	76
handi	21	18.5	38.4	30.5	70
handi	20	16	30.5	23	40
jar	19	15	33	36	30
jar	17	–	–	–	–
jar	22	–	–	–	–
lid	32.5	–	31.5	7.1	140
milk boiling pot	29	27.5	32.8	17.5	90
muri roaster	57	–	51	18	120
muri roaster	63	–	–	–	–
muri chhaka khola (sieve)	31.5	–	36	20.5	80
hola (offering pot)	13	–	–	–	–
rice pot	22	18.5	30.9	26	52
huluni (ritual basin)	32	–	35.5	22.5	70
habishyi khola (ritual bowl)	22	20	30	11.2	100
habishyi khola (ritual bowl)	26	–	25	13.5	86
habishyi khola (ritual bowl)	23	–	–	–	–
pujar ghat (worship pot)	18.5	14.5	28.6	28	40
pujar ghat (worship pot)	14	–	22.1	21.1	–
tawa	29	–	26.5	6	130
daba (basin)	50	–	44.5	47	80
daba	45	–	38.5	31.5	90
daba	36	–	–	–	–
daba	47	–	–	–	–
vegetable pot	36	31.5	38	19	100
vegetable pot	20	18	29	11.2	94
vegetable pot	29	27.5	32	17.5	90
water jar	19	15	32.4	35.5	30
tijel (pot for boiling milk)	29	–	–	–	–
tijel	20	–	–	–	–

The earlier measurement comes from four potter families: not all had all the shapes present at the same time. This does not mean that a particular household specializes in a particular product. One household was also making stoves and grinders.

Jalpara (Mangalkot PS)

The soil for pottery is acquired from the local lake, the slip is bought from Ilmati Bajar and also produced from *murum* (red lateritic soil). The raw material for the slip also comes from Guskara which is also the market for finished products. The products are described Table 2.11.

Ichchhabat (Mangalkot PS)

This village has 110 potter households. All work full time. The clay for pottery comes from a pond. The slip is made with material from Rampurhat. The pots are mostly handmade (Table 2.12).

Khajurdihi (Katwa PS)

In this village the potters collect earth from the field and the red soil for slip comes from Ahmadpur. Here too most of the pots are handmade or on mould (Table 2.13). The market is at Katwa.

TABLE 2.11: Ceramic types from Jalpara

pot type	*rim (in cm.)*	*neck (in cm.)*	*body (in cm.)*	*height (in cm.)*	*opening (in cm.)*
charan (basin)	31	–	31.5	13.4	104
charan	26		–	–	–
handi-kadai (beef pot)	26	19.5	40	33.5	36
date pitcher	15	–	–	–	–
frying pan	23	–	–	8.2	110
frying pan	59	–	55	20.2	110
handi	23	21	31.6	24	70
handi	30	27.5	33	18	82
muri tola (roaster)	91	–	–	–	–
khapuri (pan/roaster)	59	–	56	20.2	112
chhaka khola (sieve)	32	–	37	21.5	80
chhaka khola	36	–	42.5	22.3	82
malsa (ritual bowl)	22	–	25	11.8	80
pujar ghat (worship pot)	16	10.9	21	19.8	40
dab (basin)	48	–	–	–	–
dab	53	–	–	–	–
water jar	14.5	10.5	32	33.5	30
water pitcher	15	10.5	32	34	20

TABLE 2.12: Ceramic types from Ichchhabat

pot type	*rim (in cm.)*	*neck (in cm.)*	*body (in cm.)*	*height (in cm.)*	*opening (in cm.)*
hola (offering bowl)	26	–	–	13.2	80
date pot	16	–	–	–	–
frying pan	33	–	30	12	100
frying pan	27	–	30	12	100
frying pan	30	–	26	13.4	100
khapuri (roaster)	57	–	52	18.8	120
chhaka khola (sieve)	32	–	–	13.5	100
handi (cooking rice & feeding cow)	21	–	28.8	23	60
tawa	29	–	27	4.9	150
dab (boiling paddy & feeding cow)	61	–	–	–	–
water pitcher	15.5	10	32.5	35	20
water pot	16	14	21.5	19.5	48

Water pitcher is made only from mid-April to mid-June (*Baishakh* and *Jaishtha* Bengali months), pot for date juice is also manufactured but was not available at that time. The commercial fry pan is double the size of domestic type. Again it was not available that time.

Shudpur (Katwa PS)

The potters bought soil and raw material from shop at Katwa. The market for the finished product is also at Katwa. The pottery in this village is mostly handmade (Table 2.14).

Gafulia Pashchimpalpara (Katwa PS)

This village also has full-time potters. The clay is acquired from the village field and lake. The colour for the slip is procured from Ahmadpur in Birbhum district. Pottery is manufactured on the wheel, in moulds and by hand (Table 2.15). The market again is at Katwa.

TABLE 2.13: Ceramic types from Khajurdihi

pot type	*rim (in cm.)*	*neck (in cm.)*	*body (in cm.)*	*height (in cm.)*	*opening (in cm.)*
dhuki (*pithe* pot Muslim)	12	8.5	23	17.6	30
curd pot	18	16.5	20	14.9	70
khuli handi (frying pan)	27	–	26	11.4	112
chhaka khola (sieve)	32	–	37.6	16.8	80
vegitable pot	21	19.5	23.5	13	100
water jar	16	14	24.5	24	36

TABLE 2.14: Ceramic types from Shudpur

pot type	rim (in cm.)	neck (in cm.)	body (in cm.)	height (in cm.)	opening (in cm.)
pithe bowl	24	–	–	7.1	120
curd pot	21	–	21	14	80
lid	15	–	13.5	9	120
rice pot	21	–	21	14	80
sara (ritual tray)	23	–	23.9	15.6	80
habishyi handi (ritual cooking pot)	13	9.5	18.5	18.2	40
tawa	26	–	26.5	6.8	130

SOUTH 24 PARGANAS

The surface elevation of this district is generally below 10 m. from the mean sea level. The land is inundated by distributaries of Ganga (De 1994). The district is bordered by the river Bhagirathi-Hugli in the west and the river Ichhamati in the east. Rivers like Bidyadhari and Piyali have lost connection with their parent stream and receive only rainwater. Further south tidal ingressions have formed several funnel shaped estuaries like Thakran, Bidya, Matla, Raymagal, etc. The soil is new alluvium with very little profile development. The soil has been categorized into five types: clayey, loamy, sandy loam, sandy soil of newly formed island and silty soil found in pockets along the distributaries.

TABLE 2.15: Ceramic types from Gafulia Pashchimpalpara

pot type	rim (in cm.)	neck (in cm.)	body (in cm.)	height (in cm.)	opening (in cm.)
liquor pot	31	27	36.5	23.1	75
beef pot	33	27.5	42	37.5	46
beef pot	31	–	36.5	23.1	70
kodai	30	–	34	13.1	110
handi	31	27	36.5	27.5	70
muri chala	62	–	–	–	–
muri chala	30.5	–	29	11.5	102
muri chhaka (sieve)	30.5	–	32	15.4	100
rice pot	31	–	36.5	23.1	70
rice pot	23	–	–	–	–
habishyi handi (ritual cooking pot)	24	–	24.5	14.9	80
daba (basin)	51	–	45	32.8	80
vegitable pot	29	–	32.4	14.7	100
vegitable pot	23	–	24.7	12.5	90
water pitcher	16	–	30	33	22

Khotir Bajar (Raydighi PS)

For making rice pot and vegetable pot, coarse sand is brought from Arambagh in Hugli district, about 150 km. away. Fine grained sand is procured from local ponds which were possibly part of abandoned channels. The ochre colour used for slip comes from Medinipur district. The source would be some 100 km. away from the village. There is another colour derived from the 'mud-stick' (insect-nest) and it is found locally. It yields a maroonish tint. The pots are made on the wheel, in moulds and is also shaped by hand (Table 2.16). The market is at Raydighi at some 20 km. distance, Kashinagar and Mitraganj at about 10 km. away.

Mandalpara (Boyargadi) (Raydighi PS)

The source of clay is in the village. The material for the slip comes from Medinipur and the black colour for painting comes from car batteries! Earlier the black colour was produced from a type of soil presently not easily available here. Pottery is wheel-made, mould-made and handmade (Table 2.17). The market is at Raydighi, Kashinagar.

The dish with obliquely cut rim is completely handmade and crude. The village also makes the 'bird nest' which is a handi with a hole in the shoulder for the bird to go in and out. These are hung from the nave of the thatched roof and are believed to bring peace.

TABLE 2.16: Ceramic types from Khotir Bajar

pot type	*rim (in cm.)*	*neck (in cm.)*	*body (in cm.)*	*height (in cm.)*	*opening (in cm.)*
pithe bowl (perforated)	23	–	–	9	104
pithe bowl (perforated)	18	–	18.5	7	110
date pitcher	13	9.5	20.5	28	26
frying pan	28.5	–	27	7.5	110
lid	12	–	–	5	110
malsa	22	20	21.5	9.5	70
malsa	18	–	20.3	13.5	70
rice pot	15	13.5	21.6	19	52
rice pot	19	17.4	25	17.5	60
mejla (basin for soaking paddy)	74	–	–	–	–
mejla	62	–	63.5	42	80
mejla	82	–	–	–	–
tijel (vegitable pot)	22	19.5	25	13	108
tijel (vegitable pot)	19	16.5	23	14.5	100
water pitcher	13	11.4	24	22.5	24
water jar	17	15.2	31	30	32

TABLE 2.17: Ceramic types from Mandalpara Boyargadi

pot type	*rim (in cm.)*	*neck (in cm.)*	*body (in cm.)*	*height (in cm.)*	*opening (in cm.)*
pither khola (bowl)	27	–	–	12	100
raser dabri (date pitcher)	14	11	14.5	14.5	44
dish	29	–	–	6.5	140
lid	13	–	–	6	120
dhan chhaka (paddy soaking pot) (see Pl. 20)	18	16.4	32.5	32.5	30
rice pot	19	16.5	28.5	23.5	60
water pitcher	15	11.2	37.5	38	20

Tantirhat (Kulpi PS)

The clay for making pots is acquired from specific fields. Sand comes from Kulpi and slip is from Diamond Harbour, a small port town on Bahagirathi-Hugli. The latter receives a lot of country boats from Medinipur district and, therefore, the clay for the slip probably comes from that region. Here too pottery is made by wheel, hand and mould (Table 2.18). The markets for the products are Amtala, Kakdwip and Diamond Harbour some 15 to 20 km. away and some items are also sold locally.

Other sizes of *mejla* are also made but were not available at that point.

Nakali (Kulpi PS)

The potters acquire clay from the fields, sand from the market at Simulberia (earlier it had to be brought from Lakshmikantapur) and material for slip is bought in Dhola, Lakshmikantapur or Jumai Laskar. All these are market places situated some 10–15 km. from the village and not the original source of raw materials. These probably have their origins in the western districts of West Bengal where a lot of coarse sand is deposited by river flowing down from the Chotanagpur plateau and soil formed from degeneration of lateritic rocks. Common products are listed in Table 2.19.

Potters also make pitcher and *tawa* which was not available during the survey. Here the raw material is from the same sources as the previous village except that the deeper red is made from insect nests and the black colour is from batteries. The market for the products of Nakali is at Lakshmikantapur.

Gabberia (Kulpi PS)

The clay is from the local field and fine sand which is also locally available. Large grained sand is brought from Bijayganj some 10 km. away, the true

TABLE 2.18: Ceramic types from Tantirhat

pot type	*rim (in cm.)*	*neck (in cm.)*	*body (in cm.)*	*height (in cm.)*	*opening (in cm.)*
pither khola (for pancakes)	26	–	–	10	90
raser dabri (date juice pitcher)	13	9	26	27	32
dhakni (lid for pancakes)	13	–	–	–	–
tal handi (palm juice pot) (see Pl. 26)	15	13.5	29	19	50
rice pot	20	–	33	25	50
sara (ritual tray)	25	–	–	6	130
malsa (ritual bowl)	20	–	24	9	82
debi ghat (ritual pot)	13	5.5	15	21	30
rachna handi (ritual pot)	12	10.5	13	8.5	56
chatu	27	–	–	4.5	140
mejla (basin)	63	–	–	–	–
water pitcher	14	10.5	27.5	26	34

TABLE 2.19: Ceramic types from Nakali

pot type	*rim (in cm.)*	*neck (in cm.)*	*body (in cm.)*	*height (in cm.)*	*opening (in cm.)*
pither khola (bowl for pancakes)	26	–	–	–	–
pither khola	23	–	–	7	114
mete (jar)	30	28.5	62	90.5	20
mete	25	24	51.5	75.5	20
dhakni (lid for covering pancakes)	13	–	–	8	84
malsa (ritual bowl)	20	–	22.5	14	80
malsa	13.5	4.5	16.5	26.5	12
mejla (basin)	80	–	–	–	–
mejla	75	–	80.5	57.5	88
mejla	55	–	–	44	80
mejla	51	–	–	42	90
mejla	43	–	–	–	–
mejla	35	–	–	33	90
mejla	26	–	–	–	–
Debi ghat (pot for worship)	13.5	–	–	–	–
Sara (offering tray)	18	–	–	–	–

TABLE 2.20: Ceramic types from Gabberia

pot type	*rim (in cm.)*	*neck (in cm.)*	*body (in cm.)*	*height (in cm.)*	*opening (in cm.)*
pither khola (for pancakes)	23	–	–	–	–
dhakni (lid for covering pancakes)	13	–	–	–	–
malsa (ritual bowl)	20	–	–	–	–
dvar ghat (ritual pot)	12	10.5	14.5	14	50
biyer ghat (ritual pot for marriage)	12	10	16.3	16.3	46
sweet *handi*	19	–	–	–	–
mejla (basin)	52	–	48.5	38	70
jaler kalsi (water pitcher)	14.5	11	26	28.7	30

TABLE 2.21: Ceramic types from Shikharbali

pot type	*rim (in cm.)*	*neck (in cm.)*	*body (in cm.)*	*height (in cm.)*	*opening (in cm.)*
date juice pot	7.5	7	10	10.5	30
sweet pot	18	16.5	20.5	13	76
water pitcher	13	11	37.5	38	20
water pitcher (used also for supporting *paniphal* plant)	15	12	32.5	35	22
mejla (basin)	44	–	–	–	–
mejla	50	–	–	–	–
mejla	60	–	–	–	–
mejla	67	–	–	–	–

source of which would be again in the western part of West Bengal. The colour for the slip is bought from local market and Bijayganj. The black colour for painting comes from black nodules present in the soil in certain pockets. The products are listed in Table 2.20. The market for the product is at Dhola, which is nearby and sweet *handis* are sold at Kolkata around 25 km. away and some articles like basins are sold at the house only.

Shikharbali (Baruipur PS)

The utensils are few (Table 2.21) but there are some other interesting objects like nests for birds. These are hung outside the house from the straw shades and shelters sparrow and pigeon. These nests, the villagers believe, would bring peace and happiness in the family. The raw material comes from similar sources as other villages. Market is at Sasan, which is nearby.

Gorerhat (Jaynagar-Majilpur PS)

This village has some potters' neighbourhoods and they specialize in a few items (Table 2.22). One makes water pots and *malsa* and the other makes water pitchers. Pitchers and basins were in the kiln and, therefore, could not be measured. Here too the black colour is procured from batteries. The raw material is obtained locally. The market is at Dakshin Barasat, located nearby.

TABLE 2.22: Ceramic types from Gorerhat

pot type	*rim (in cm.)*
malsa (ritual bowl)	20
water jar	19
water jar	22

Jugigora Palpara (Jaynagar Majilpur PS)

The clay is again local. The sand is procured from the local river or a palaeochannel. Most of the pots are being made by hand and mould (Table 2.23). The market is at Jaynagar Majilpur.

Some potters sell their products in Kolkata. But these are mostly the special products like pots for sweets and curd, or pot for plant.

MALDA

The river Mahananda bisects the district from north to south. To its east is the undulating Barind surface of Pleistocene age. Tangan and Punarbhaba rivers flow through this region. To the west the land is divided by Kalindri River, possibily an old channel of the river Ganga. North of Kalindri is marshy Tal (backwater) and the south is well drained Diara formation characterized by the braided stream of the Ganga. These are mostly new alluvium belonging to middle to late Holocene. Barind consists of deep clayey loam, Tal consists of clay to clay loam while the Diara is sandy loam (Sengupta 1969).

Kadubari (Gazol PS)

The soil is brought by truck from nearby source like Rashidpur or dug out from field locally. The sand is from the Aral River. The material for the slip comes from Gazole. The market is also at Gazole. Products are listed in Table 2.24.

Krishnapalli (Gazol PS)

Here too the soil is locally procured. The sand is bought from Gazole and mixed with ash for tempering the paste. The raw material for the slip is also from Gazole as in earlier cases. In these villages the older alluvium of Barind surface is used for the slip and is available nearby. Pottery is made on wheel, mould and by hand (Table 2.25). The products are sold locally within the village or at Gazole.

TABLE 2.23: Ceramic types from Jugigora Palpara

pot type	*rim (in cm.)*
date pot (see Pl. 18)	13
malsa	20
basin	80
basin	35

TABLE 2.24: Ceramic types from Kadubari

pot type	*rim (in cm.)*	*neck (in cm.)*	*body (in cm.)*	*height (in cm.)*	*opening (in cm.)*
frying pan	40.5	–	43	16.2	114
handi	26.5	25	26.5	16	80
lid	20	–	19.5	8.8	140
lid	11	–	–	4.5	100
muri bhaja khola (roaster)	40.5	38	41.2	18.5	100
muri siever	40.5	38.5	43	21	94
hara (paddy soaking pot)	27	21	36.5	34	42
rice pot	25.5	20.5	39.5	38	40
rice pot	16.5	13.5	21.5	16.5	60
malsa (ritual bowl)	26	26.5	28	16	80
ritual pot	7	4.7	7	8.8	30
tawa	36.5	–	31	11	120
tawa	31.5	–	–	8	120
water pitcher	14.5	10	29.3	31	20
water pitcher	16	9.5	39	41.5	20
water pitcher	12	7.5	22	24	30

Here some amount of specialization in shapes was noticed among the potters' households. Each potter family specializes in a few types, though they might sell a few more types which they do not produce by acquiring them from those who do. There is also some difference in shapes and

TABLE 2.25: Ceramic types from Krishnapalli

pot type	*rim (in cm.)*	*neck (in cm.)*	*body (in cm.)*	*height (in cm.)*	*opening (in cm.)*
liquor pot	39	32.5	47	42	56
kadai (frying pan)	27	–	–	–	–
frying pan	32	–	30	14	100
lid (for rice pot)	24	–	22	7.5	124
lid	26	–	22.5	8	120
muri roaster	31	26	35	16	90
muri sieve	18	15	19.5	12	60
hara (paddy soaking pot)	30	26.2	30	18	80
hara	30	–	30	16.5	82
palm juice pot	28.5	25.5	36	18	42
rice pot	23	17.5	32	30.5	34
rice pot	18	15	21.5	16.5	60
tawa	30	–	27.5	7.5	140
basin	52.5	–	60	29.3	90
basin	62	–	59.5	29.5	100
vegetable pot	36	31.5	41	22	108
water pitcher	16	10	34.5	37	20

Table 2.26: Ceramic types from Mathurapur

pot type	rim (in cm.)	neck (in cm.)	body (in cm.)	height (in cm.)	opening (in cm.)
muri roaster	30	26	28.5	17	90
muri sieve	30	27.5	31.5	18.5	90
rice pot	27	22.8	36.5	35.5	50
tawa	30	–	27	8	130
tawa (for Muslims)	30	27.5	28	12	108

sizes of the water pitchers though the rim size is broadly uniform. Two kinds of wine preparing vessels were noticed. One is a rice *handi* with a large perforation on the bottom for producing rice wine and the other is a pitcher tied to the palmyra palm for collecting juice for *tadi*.

Mathurapur Palpara (English Bazar PS)

The soil is bought from Manikchak and sand from Narayanpur, both are located nearby. The colour comes from the adjoining state of Bihar. These were applied on an off-white kind of earth colour available locally. Here too the pottery is made on wheel, mould and by hand (Table 2.26). The market is at Mathurapur.

Bamunduli (Phulbaria) (English Bazar PS)

Pottry types are given in Table 2.27. There are differences in shape of the *handis*. The difference between the *handi* and the *kadai* is minor.

The soil comes from nearby. The material for slip comes from Bihar. The market for the products is extensive. The pots are sold locally, at Malda and also in Koch Bihar at a distance of around 300 km. The rice pots are occasionally also brought from Narhatta (located nearby) and sold here.

TABLE 2.27: Ceramic types from Bamunduli

pot type	rim (in cm.)	neck (in cm.)	body (in cm.)	height (in cm.)	opening (in cm.)
date pitcher	13	10.5	24.5	27	26
Kadai (frying pan)	24	20.5	26	16	70
handi (for *habishyi* or ritual food)	17	14.5	18.5	11.5	72
handi (for curd)	13	–	–	–	–
lid	20.5	–	19.1	11	120
muri roaster	30	26.5	31.5	20	80
palm juice pot	13	12	14.5	19	40
rice pot	23	19	27.6	21	60

(*Contd.*)

TABLE 2.27: (*contd.*)

pot type	*rim (in cm.)*	*neck (in cm.)*	*body (in cm.)*	*height (in cm.)*	*opening (in cm.)*
rice pot	18	16	21	15.5	60
malsa (ritual bowl)	17	14	17.1	11	74
malsa	17	14.4	17	11	80
ritual pot	7.5	5.4	14	15	28
ritual pot	8	65	9	9.5	40
ritual pot	13	11.6	16	11.3	60
sweet pot	16.5	18	20	15.5	70
water pitcher	13.5	–	–	–	–
water pitcher	13	–	–	–	–
water pitcher	12	6.5	28	31	20

CONCLUSION

This survey reveals a range of products manufactured by potter households. It also reveals how raw materials are acquired and finished products reach the consumers. Some villages make only a few objects while some others make a wide range. The basic clay is almost always local, within 5 km., and sometimes supplemented by clay brought in from a little farther away. However other ingredients like that of slip and temper can be brought from a long distance.

The markets for these products are again very diverse. The selling may happen locally at the village level markets or even bought from the houses. Some of the products would go to the larger village markets where products from different villages may be sold. The products may even go to the nearest small town. The potters may directly sell their product to the consumer or to a trader owning a shop. Most often the latter are from potter's community. Some niche products might make their way to the large town—sold to the sweet shops or to the general urban population. But sometimes pots move very far to reach their consumers like going all the way from Malda to Koch Bihar. Pottery from West Bengal makes its way, as far as, to Pune in Maharashtra.

3

Morphometry and Formal Variation

COMPARATIVE MORPHOMETRY

ARCHAEOLOGICAL POTTERY is usually classified on the basis of measurements, shape, paste, function, surface features, technique, etc. More often than not these attributes have to be obtained from shards. These are usually substantiated by referring to similar types across the site and within the cultural boundary. The classification of pottery according to morphology is based on the assumption that shapes of vessels are based on the intended function they perform. It is, however, accepted that there is more to a vessel's shape and size than function. Even function does not have only a single aspect. Ideational factors and other cultural factors give rise to variation in shape and size. It is with the aim of understanding cultural differences and the association with form and size that the survey work was undertaken and analysis of ethnographic data was conducted.

The dimensions of some common forms like *handi*, basin, frying pan and pitcher, etc. (discussed below) from the villages mentioned earlier are analysed. Then similar shapes with different functions are compared and contrasted. Lastly, regional variations are discussed to assess the impact of local cultural dimensions on functional forms.

These analyses were done with the help of very simple statistics like correlation matrix, box plot and multidimensional display. These were done to reveal patterns, if any, in the data concerned. The aim is to see the range in the size of each type, relationship between different parts and opening of the vessel, difference in size in different regions and a comparison between similar types of vessels.

RELATIONSHIP AMONG DIFFERENT PARTS OF THE VESSELS

The function of a vessel is considered to be associated with its shape. Classification into bowl, dish, or jar is done by measuring the proportions of different parts like rim, neck, body (i.e. the diameter of these parts) and height. As noted earlier, the simplicity of the process makes it a very easy formula. But many times, when applying to real situations, like assigning function to fragments belonging to different age, this method is found to be rigid and culture specific. For example, in the context of South Asia, the height of the Harappan dish is 1/6 of maximum body diameter (Dales and Kenoyer 1986) but for Early Historic period it is about 1/3 of maximum body diameter. One might consider a more flexible approach. Correlation between various parts is considered here because it gives only a picture of relationship between them. In the present ethnographic context, the functions of all shapes are known. Therefore, it is possible to correlate variations in size of components to function. All pots performing same function from different regions are grouped together without the consideration of village or district. This allowed some amount of variation in dataset giving a degree of flexibility to morphometry in a fixed time frame within a reasonably homogenous cultural community spread over different physiographic regions. But this should not be attempted without an idea of variability within each of the components. Therefore, a general distribution of measurement of diameters of different parts and the angle of opening is also presented.

Basin

Rim diameter—lower hinge 43 cm., median 50 cm., upper hinge 58 cm., maximum 82 cm., minimum 26 cm.

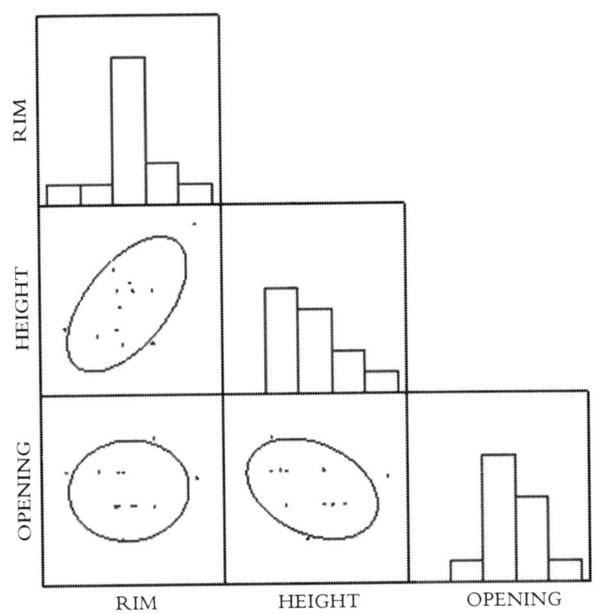

FIGURE 3.1: Correlation matrix of basin

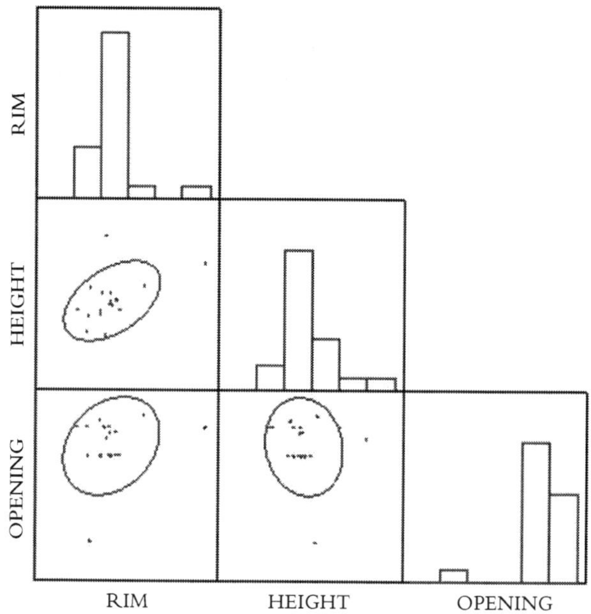

FIGURE 3.2: Correlation matrix of frying pan

Height—lower hinge 32 cm., median 40 cm., upper hinge 43 cm., maximum 57.5 cm., minimum size 29.5 cm.

Opening (angle between edge of base and edge of mouth)—lower hinge 80°, median 84°, upper hinge 90° maximum 100°, minimum 70°.

Scatter plot shows that rim diameter and opening angle are not correlated. Rim diameter and height are positively correlated while opening angle to height is negatively correlated or very loosely correlated.

Distribution curves are all normal with rim diameter and height showing strong central tendency. But the opening is platykurtic.

This basic statistic shows that the basin is usually a large size vessel with a preference for a 50 cm. rim diameter. It is a vessel for short time storage for hay or used for soaking paddy but also one with relatively easy access and often used to feed cows. Here the measure of the opening is important and is, therefore, not correlated to increase or decrease in the size of the vessel except loosely with height.

Frying pan

Rim diameter—lower hinge 26 cm., median 29 cm. and upper hinge 30 cm., maximum size 59 cm. and minimum size 20 cm.

Height—lower hinge 12 cm., median 13 cm., upper hinge 15 cm., maximum size 25 cm. and minimum size 7.5 cm.

Opening angle—Lower hinge 100°, median 106°, upper hinge 110°, maximum 114° and minimum 70°.

Distribution curved of the opening is skewed to the left. All the component parts are leptokurtic.

Scatter plot matrix shows loose correlation between rim diameter and height.

The distribution shows that there is less difference between the lower hinge and the upper hinge for all the component parts. This together with leptokurtic curves show that there is a general standardized size. The opening is obviously the key feature as it is a frying vessel. However, preference for particular depth is suggested by only 3 cm. variation between the lower and upper hinge. Too much depth would lead to wastage of oil, the cooking medium. Therefore, an increase in size means only increase in size of rim.

Muri roaster

Rim diamter—lower hinge 42 cm., median 57 cm., upper hinge 62 cm., maximum size 91 cm. and minimum is 29 cm.

Body diameter—lower hinge 31.5 cm., median 41 cm., upper hinge 52 cm., maximum size is 56 cm. and minimum is 28.5 cm.

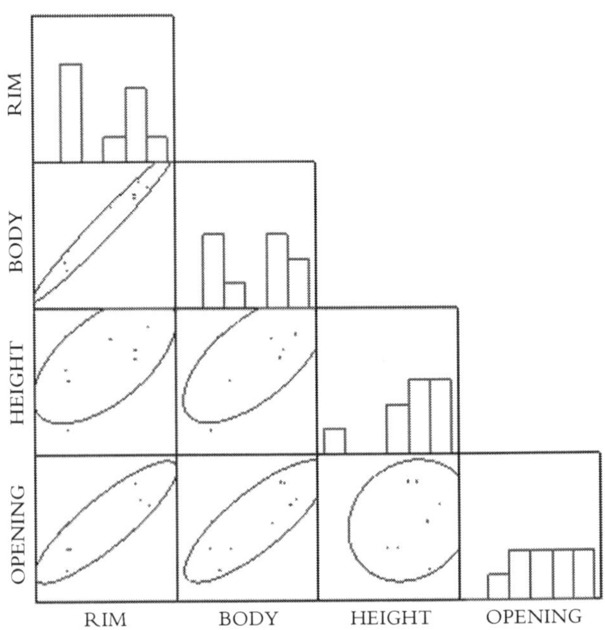

FIGURE 3.3: Correlation matrix of *muri* roaster

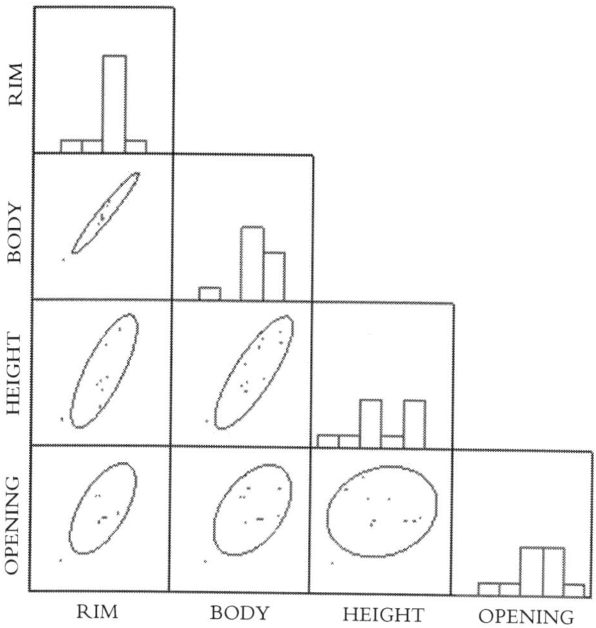

FIGURE 3.4: Correlation matrix of *muri* sieve

Height—lower hinge is 17 cm. median 18.5 cm., upper hinge is 20 cm., maximum size 21 cm. and minimum 11.5 cm.

Opening angle (base to mouth)—lower hinge 90°, median 102°, upper hinge 112°, maximum 120° and minimum 80°.

Distribution curve of the body diameter and height slightly skewed to left while rim and opening are almost normal.

There is a strong positive correlation between body and rim diameters and positive correlation between rim diameter and opening and body diameter and opening. Height and rim diameter and height and body diameter showed weak positive correlation.

This vessel also tends to follow a size standard and tends to the larger size. This vessel also gives importance to accessibility to the vessel interior. At the same time of affords more volume than a frying pan. But smaller vessels would have smaller openings, unlike that of the frying pan.

Muri sieve

Rim diameters—lower hinge 30 cm., median 30 cm., upper hinge 32 cm., maximum 40.5 cm. and minimum is 18 cm.

Body diameters—lower hinge 31.7 cm., median 33 cm., upper hinge 37.3 cm., maximum 43 cm. and minimum 19.5 cm.

Height—lower hinge 14.5 cm., median 16.5 cm., upper hinge 20.5 cm. maximum 22.3 cm. and minimum is 12 cm.

Opening angle—lower hinge 80°, median 86°, and upper hinge 94°, maximum 100° and minimum 60°.

The distribution curve of rim is almost normal, height and body are slightly skewed to the left and opening is leptokurtic.

Scatter plot again shows strong positive correlation between rim and body diameters, positive correlation between rim diameters and height and body diameters and height and weak positive correlation of opening with rim and body diameters.

The basic statistical analysis shows that there is a tendency towards a standard size as suggested by small differences between the lower and the upper hinge. The importance of proportions is emphasized as most of the component parts are positively correlated except the opening. This is because of the necessity to prevent the contents from spilling out easily when shaken.

Rice pot

Rim diameter—lower hinge 19 cm., median 20 cm., upper hinge 24 cm., maximum 31 cm. and minimum is 15 cm.

Neck diameter—lower hinge is 15.75 cm., median is 17.5 cm., upper hinge 21 cm., maximum 25.6 cm. and minimum is 13.5 cm.

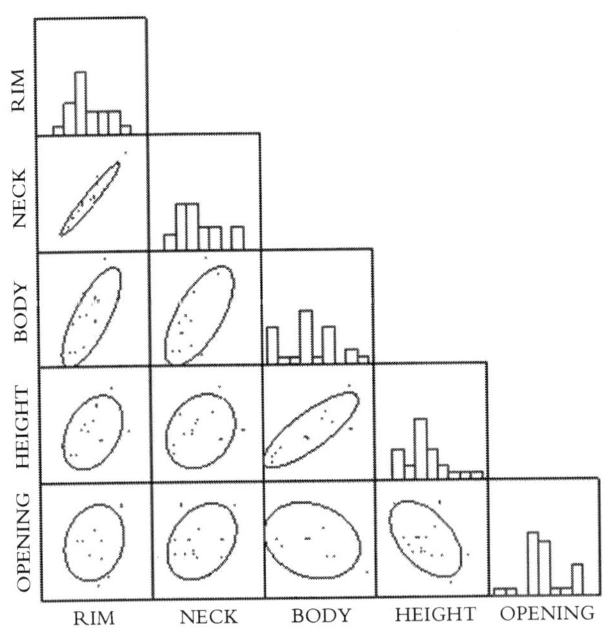

FIGURE 3.5: Correlation matrix of rice pot

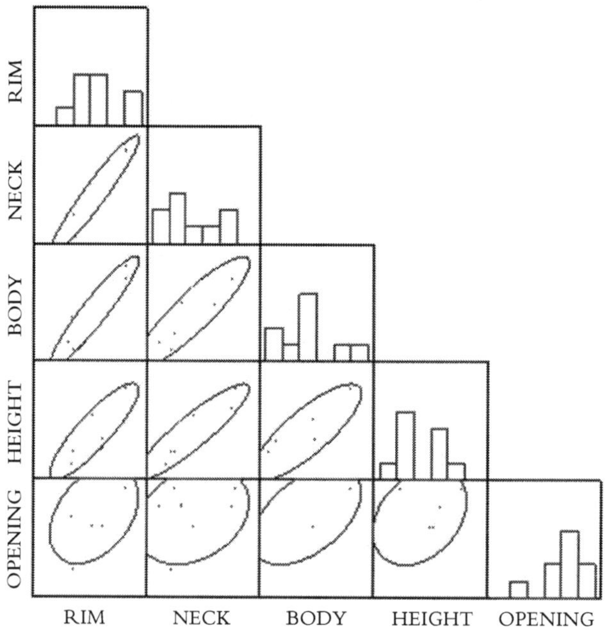

FIGURE 3.6: Correlation matrix of vegetable cooking pot

Body diameter—lower hinge 25 cm., median 28.5 cm., upper hinge 32 cm., maximum 25.5 cm., minimum 13.5 cm.

Height—lower hinge 19.5 cm., median 22 cm., upper hinge 32 cm., maximum is 38 cm. and minimum 14 cm.

Opening angle—lower hinge 50°, median 60°, upper hinge 60°, maximum 80° and minimum 34°.

The distribution curve for the rim and opening are leptokurtic. All the aspects other than the rim are slightly skewed to the right.

Scatter plot shows strong positive correlation of body with rim, neck and height, strong positive correlation of rim with neck. The opening is not correlated with any other aspect.

This container is used for boiling rice, and a narrow neck would make it more fuel efficient; it would be easier to separate the starch from rice after the boiling is over.

Vegetable cooking pot

Rim diameter—lower hinge 22 cm., median 26 cm., upper hinge 29 cm., maximum 36 cm. and minimum 19 cm.

Body diameter—lower hinge 24.7 cm., median 30 cm., upper hinge 32 cm., maximum 41 cm. and minimum 21 cm.

Height—lower hinge 13 cm., median 14.6 cm., upper hinge 18 cm., maximum 22 cm. and minimum 11 cm.

Opening angle—lower hinge 90°, median 97° and upper hinge 100°, maximum 108° and minimum 70°.

Distribution curve shows that rim is normal, neck, body and height are skewed to the right and opening to the left. This suggests tendency towards maximizing the opening.

Scatter plot shows strong positive correlations between neck, rim and body diameters. It also shows positive correlation between height and other parts except opening from the base. Opening from the base is not correlated to any other aspect.

A vegetable pot would need to accommodate shallow frying as well as boiling. It has a large rim diameter (around 26 cm.) but is also restricted by the constricted neck, as a result the opening is not as large as it would be otherwise.

Water pitcher

Rim diameter—lower hinge 13 cm., median 14.5 cm., upper hinge 16 cm., maximum 19 cm. and minimum is 12 cm.

Neck diameter—lower hinge 10 cm., median 10.5 cm., upper hinge 11.2 cm., maximum 13 cm. and minimum 6.5 cm.

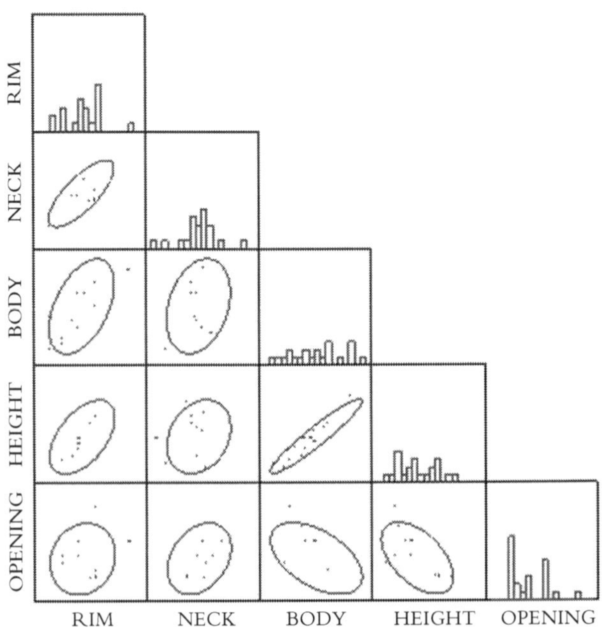

FIGURE 3.7: Correlation matrix of water pitcher

Body diameter—lower hinge 26.75 cm., median 30 cm., upper hinge 33.55 cm., maximum 39 cm. and minimum 22 cm.

Height—lower hinge 27 cm., median 30 cm., upper hinge 36 cm., maximum is 43 cm. and minimum 22.5 cm.

Opening angle—lower hinge 20°, median 24°, upper hinge 30°, maximum 40° and minimum 20°.

Distribution curve shows height is leptokurtic and slightly skewed to the right. Rim diameter is also slightly skewed to the right. Neck and body diameters have normal distribution. The opening angle is skewed to the right but platykurtic.

Correlation matrix revealed positive relation between height and body diameter and between neck and rim diameters. That between opening and body diameter is positive but weak and that between opening angle and height is loosely negative. Neck shows very little correlation with opening, height or body.

Though there is some variation in opening from the base and rim diameter the emphasis is towards a small size. The height shows strongest central tendency among all the aspects. Pitcher is not just for storage but also used for transportation. It is carried on the hip or waist by women. Therefore, height is standardized towards the low side. As it is meant for carrying liquid, the opening from the base is kept small but platykurtic curve shows no central tendency within that range.

Water jar

Rim diameter—lower hinge 16 cm., median 16.75 cm., upper hinge 19 cm., maximum 28 cm. and minimum 13 cm.

Neck diameter—lower hinge 14 cm., median 14.4 cm., upper hinge 15.2 cm., maximum 23 cm. and minimum 10.5 cm.

Body diameter—lower hinge 24.5 cm., median 31 cm., upper hinge 32.4 cm., maximum 46 cm. minimum 21 cm.

Height—lower hinge 24 cm., median 30 cm., upper hinge 35 cm., maximum 50 cm. and minimum 19 cm.

Opening angle—lower hinge 30°, median 32°, upper hinge 36°, maximum 48° and minimum 20°.

Distribution curves of all except that of the opening are skewed to the right. The curve for the opening from the base is platykurtic and skewed a little to left.

The correlation matrix shows that rim diameter is correlated to the neck diameter and loosely correlated to body diameter and height. Height and body diameter are strongly correlated. Opening angle has weak negative correlation with body diameter and height.

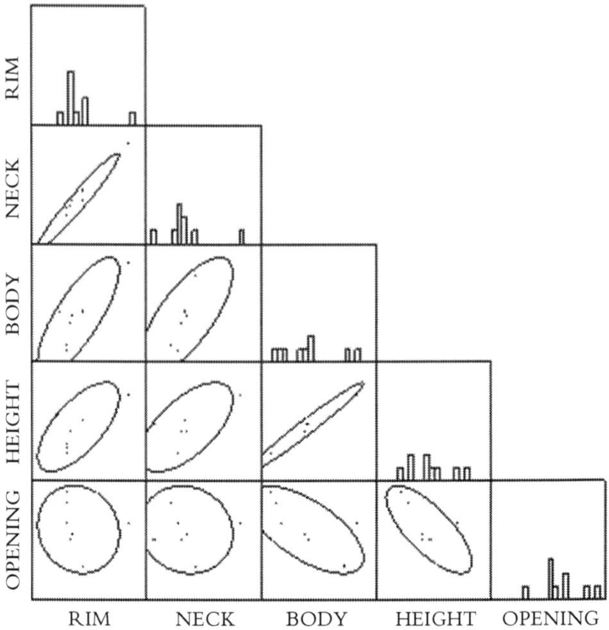

FIGURE 3.8: Correlation matrix of water jar

Water jar is a storage vessel and not used for transport. Therefore, unlike the pitcher, it is found in various sizes. Distribution curve, however, suggests that large jars are relatively few. The correlation matrix, together with the distribution, suggests that size of rim and neck diameters varies little. The difference in size is achieved by change in body diameter and height. The opening loosely depends on the size of the jar and unlike the pitcher it must accommodate a scoop for withdrawing water towards a wide mouth.

Ritual bowl

Rim diameter—lower hinge 20 cm., median 22 cm., upper hinge 25 cm., maximum 30 cm. and minimum 15 cm.

Body diameter—lower hinge 22 cm., median 24.5 cm., upper hinge 28 cm., maximum 32 cm. and minimum 17 cm.

Height—lower hinge 11 cm., median 11.8 cm., upper hinge 14.9 cm., maximum 20 cm., minimum 9 cm.

Opening angle—lower hinge 80°, median 80°, upper hinge 82°, maximum 100° and minimum 70°.

Distribution curves show rim and body diameters are normal with central tendency, opening has platykurtic curve and height is skewed to right.

The scatter plot shows positive correlation of rim diameter with body diameter and height and week positive correlation of body diameter and height. Opening from the base shows no correlation.

The vessel tends to be made in a definite size. It is used for cooking and serving on specific occasions, and is not used every day. The opening suggests moderate accessibility to the pot interior.

Ritual pot

Rim diameter—lower hinge 12 cm., median 13 cm., upper hinge 14 cm., maximum 18.5 cm. and minimum 4 cm.

Neck diameter—lower hinge 5.5 cm., median 9.6 cm., upper hinge 11 cm., maximum 14.5 cm. and minimum 3.5 cm.

Body diameter—lower hinge 14 cm., median 16.3 cm., upper hinge 19.5 cm., maximum 28.6 cm. and minimum 4.5 cm.

Height—lower hinge 10.65 cm., median 16.3 cm., upper hinge 19.9 cm., maximum 28 cm. and minimum 4.5 cm.

Opening angle—lower hinge 40°, median 40°, upper hinge 50°, maximum 80° and minimum 12°.

The distribution curve for the body diameter is normal and height is towards leptokurtic, the rim is slightly skewed to left and the diameter of the neck and the opening angle is skewed to right.

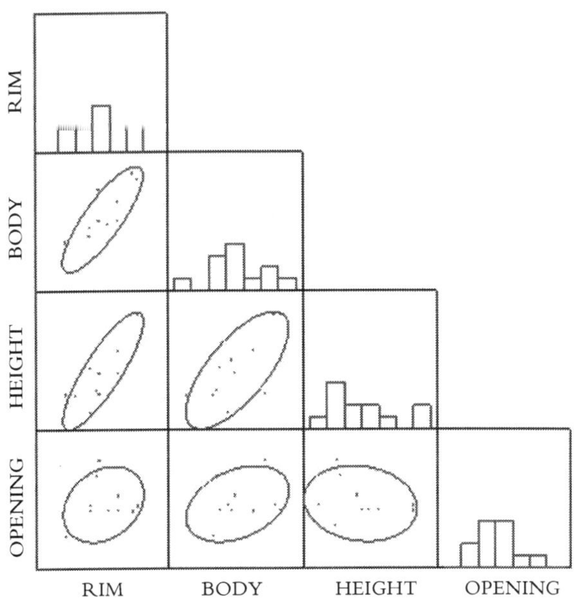

FIGURE 3.9: Correlation matrix of ritual bowl

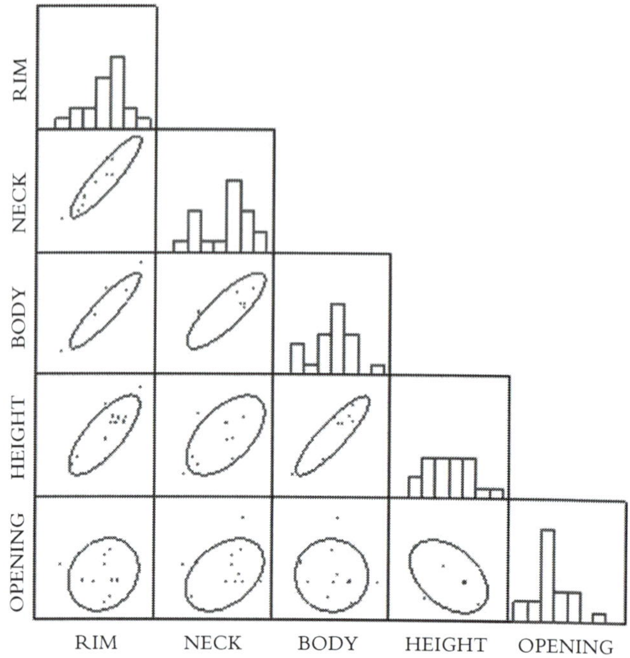

FIGURE 3.10: Correlation matrix of ritual pot

The scatter plot shows rim, neck and body diameters and height positively correlated, while angle and height have weak correlation and there is no correlation between rim diameter and opening angle. The ritual pots are mostly small sized with narrow openings as suggested by skewed curve of the neck diameter to the right. Increase of body parts of the pot are not related to the size of the opening.

Handi

Rim diameter—lower hinge 21 cm., median 23 cm., upper hinge 28.5 cm., maximum 40 cm., minimum 17 cm.

Neck diameter—lower hinge 17 cm., median 22.5 cm., upper hinge 27 cm., maximum 37 cm., minimum 17 cm.

Body diameter—lower hinge 28.5 cm., median 30.5 cm., upper hinge 34.75 cm., maximum 46.5 cm., minimum 18.5 cm.

Height—lower hinge 17.65 cm., median 23 cm., upper hinge 25.75 cm., maximum 33 cm. and minimum 13 cm.

Opening angle—lower hinge 67°, median 70°, upper hinge 74°, maximum 82° and minimum 40°.

The scatter plot shows that rim and neck diameters and body diameter and height have strong positive correlations. The rim, neck and body diameters too are positively correlated. The correlation between opening and other aspects are very loose.

Distribution curves show rim diameters, neck diameters, height are skewed to the right, body diameter is leptokurtic and opening angle is skewed to the left. The curve for neck diameter is leptokurtic.

The parts are correlated positively except the opening angle, which is mildly negative in correlation with all. The opening is restricted as this vessel is used for boiling food items, but leans towards a larger size. This may be because it is more a general purpose vessel than rice pot or vegetable pot. But it is for a standard volume as reflected by leptokurtic distribution curve of body.

Roasting platter (*tawa*)

Rim diameter—lower hinge 29 cm., median 29 cm., upper hinge 30 cm., maximum 36.5 cm., minimum 21 cm.

Height—lower hinge 6 cm., median 7.5 cm., upper hinge 8 cm., maximum 15 cm. and minimum 4.5 cm.

Opening angle—lower hinge 130°, median 130°, upper hinge 140°, maximum 150° and minimum 120°.

Distribution curve is leptokurtic for all the variables.

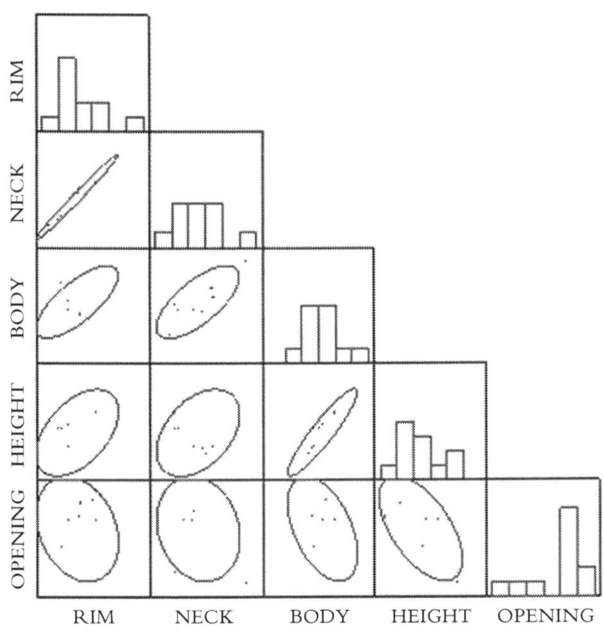

FIGURE 3.11: Correlation matrix of *handi*

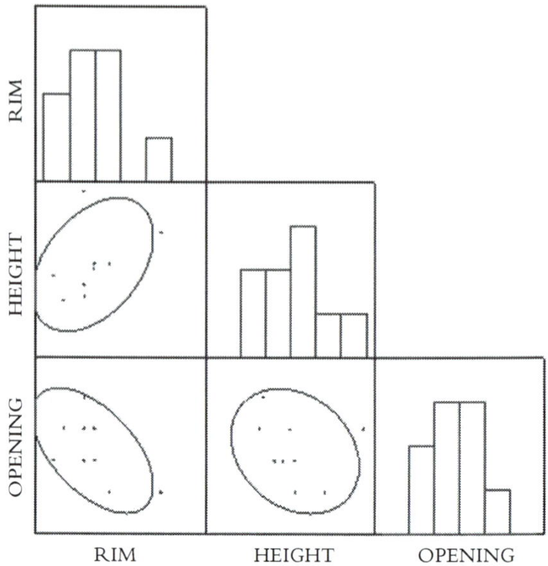

FIGURE 3.12: Correlation matrix of roaster platter

Scatter plot shows very loose positive correlation between rim and height. But correlation between opening and rim and opening is towards negative.

A standardization of size is noticed. For this form too, the surface area is the most important. The depth or height in this case has much to do with the manufacturing process (see page __).

Lid

Rim diameter—lower hinge 12.5 cm., median 13 cm., upper hinge 21.75 cm., maximum 32.5 cm. and minimum 10.5 cm.

Height—lower hinge 5 cm., median 7 cm., upper hinge 8 cm., maximum 11 cm. and minimum 3 cm.

Opening angle—lower hinge 110°, median 120°, upper hinge 130°, maximum 140° and minimum 84°.

Distribution curve shows rim diameter and opening from the base are skewed to right and left respectively and height is normal. But none shows strong central tendency.

Scatter plot shows that opening from the base and rim diameter are correlated positively but the relationship is loose.

There are many different sizes of lid for specific vessels and purpose. But lids for narrow mouthed vessels are predominantly present. Therefore, the distribution curve for the rim diameter is skewed to the right.

Jar

Rim diameter—lower hinge 18 cm., median 22 cm., upper hinge 27.5 cm., maximum 67 cm., minimum 16.5 cm.

Neck diameter—lower hinge 16.5 cm., median 24 cm., upper hinge 28.5 cm., maximum 65 cm., minimum 15 cm.

Body diameter—lower hinge 33 cm., median 51.5 cm., upper hinge 62 cm., maximum 130.5 cm., minimum 26.5 cm.

Height—lower hinge 36 cm., median 75.5 cm., upper hinge 90.5 cm., maximum 165.5 cm. and minimum 26.5 cm.

Opening angle—lower hinge 20°, median 20°, upper hinge 20°, maximum 30° and minimum 20°.

Scatter plot shows that all the aspects except the opening are strongly correlated.

The distribution curves of all the aspects are skewed to the right signifying that not too many large jars are found. Also, none of the aspects show any centralizing tendency, which suggests a lot of variation in size.

COMPARATIVE MORPHOMETRY OF VESSEL TYPES

A comparison was made between vessels with similar features but different functions. The purpose was to gauge the morphometric differences among these types. Can such differences be meaningfully used in the case of

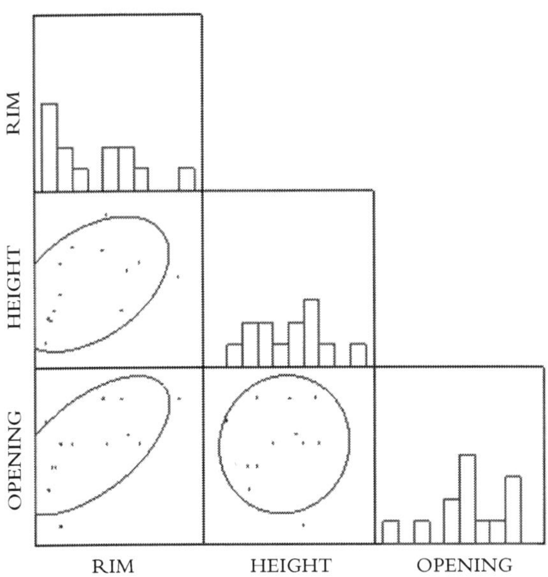

FIGURE 3.13: Correlation matrix of lid

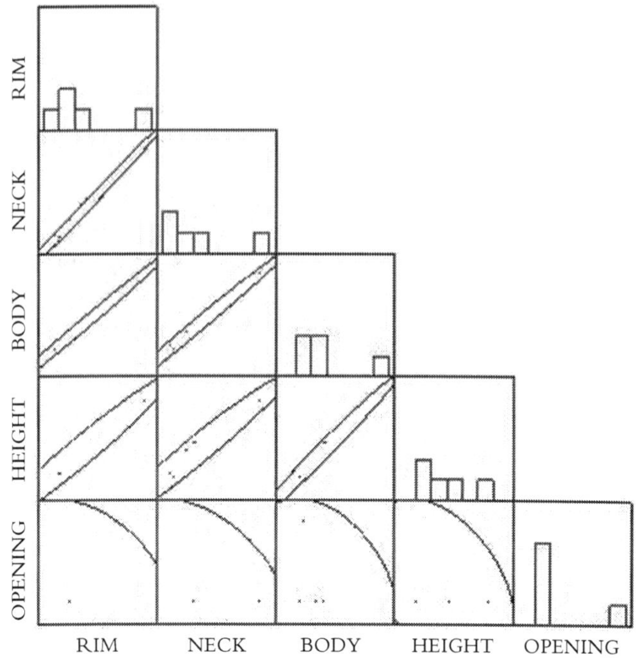

FIGURE 3.14: Correlation matrix of jar

archaeological ceramics? Here median value is taken as standard size for different parts. It is, however, possible that median value of, for example, rim and neck, may not actually occur in any single vessel. These were then subjected to multivariate parallel coordinated display to obtain graphical representation of shapes which can be easily compared.

Comparison between narrow necked vessels

The most prominent feature in this group is the opening angle. For water jars the line holds steady, for date (juice) pots it moves up and for the water pitcher it dips. For the jar the dip is sharper.

The diameter of rim of date pots are the lowest, followed by that of water pitcher and water jar. The jar is the largest, with the rim diameter varying between 20 and 30 cm.

The diameter of the neck is the least in water pitcher followed by the date (juice) pot. Water jar varies between 10 and 20 cm. and the range for jar is about 15–30 cm.

The body diameter of date pots is the smallest. The water pitcher, which is most standardized of the four, is a little larger, 30 cm. It is followed by the water jar which has its median closer to pitcher. The jar has the largest body and also the widest range with the median lying at 51 cm. mark.

The date pots have the lowest height, followed by the pitcher. Both have shown maximum standardization. The jar is the tallest and as in the case of the body, it also has the longest range.

The date (juice) pots have the largest opening, 30°–50°. The date pitcher ranges between 20° and 40°. Water pitcher ranges in the 20s, water jar in 30s and the jar is steady on 20°.

Date pots are used for hanging on the date palm to collect the juice. So they are smaller than pitchers in body and height. Mouths are small so that birds may not drink from them to collect sap. The neck of the pitcher is narrower to restrict outflow of water because it is used in short distance transport balanced on the waist of women. The opening of the jar

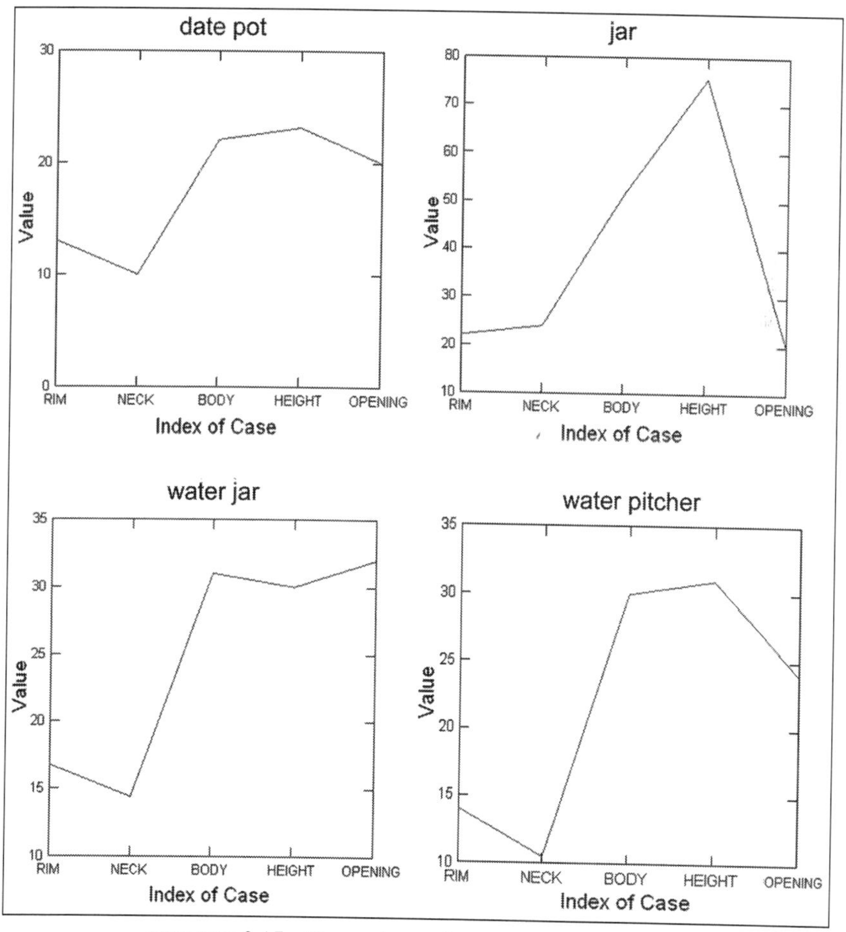

FIGURE 3.15: Dimensions of narrow necked vessels

is also restricted for longer storage. The water jar, used only for storage, has a larger opening than pitcher.

The jar is a very distinct category which can be easily recognized in archaeological contexts, and the water jar, water pitcher and date pot are similar. With respect to that of the water pitcher, the rim diameter of the date pot is less but the neck is proportionately more as suggested by a relatively gentle slope between rim and neck. Both the rim and the neck diameters of the water jar are more than that of the water pitcher and the date pot. The proportions of all the other parts are closer to that of date pot.

Comparison between open mouthed deep to medium deep vessels

The line for the basin from rim to body is flat and dips slightly on reaching height. For the *muri* roaster the dip from rim to body and body to height

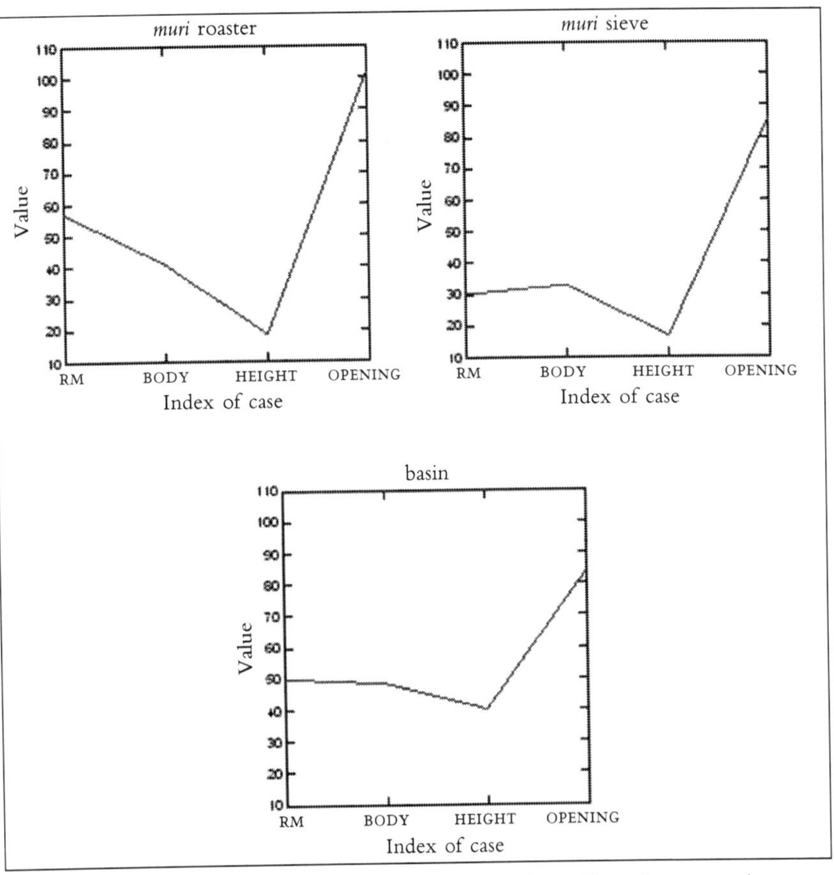

FIGURE 3.16: Dimensions of open-mouthed, medium deep vessels

is steep. For the sieve the line goes up from rim to body and then plunges down at height.

The rim diameter of *muri* sieve hovers at around 30 cm. The *muri* roaster is of much larger size ranging between 40 and 60 cm. with kurtosis spreading below 30 cm. and over 90 cm. The size of basin ranges between 40 and 60 cm. with kurtosis stretching below 30 cm. and above 80 cm.

The body diameter of *muri* sieve ranges in the 30s and roaster 30–50 cm. The basin has much longer range, from the 30s to the 80s.

The height of basin is also much greater ranging from the 30s to the 60s while *muri* sieve and roaster are mostly below the 20s.

The opening of the roaster is the largest ranging from 90° to 110°. The sieve range between 80° and 90° with kurtosis stretching down to 60°. Basin ranges mostly in the 80°s.

In archaeological context the greatest probability is to find just the rim and body. In that case the graph is very suggestive as all the three types show very different slopes between the rim and the body diameters. *Muri* sieve and roaster are both specialized vessels. But the presence of similar functional type is not ruled out. A roaster has much wider rim compared to its body than the other two. For the sieve the body is comparatively larger.

Comparison between shallow open mouthed vessels

Here all the three aspects are required to distinguish the types. The graph shows *tawa* and the frying pan show a similar dip in the line from the rim to the height but rise from the height to the opening is steeper in case of *tawa*. The line joining the rim and height slope gradually in case of the lid.

The lids have the largest range in rim diameter with most measuring in 10s but upper end of the kurtosis spreading to early 30s. Frying pan ranges from 20s to early 30s and the majority lies in the late 20s. The cake bowl (not shown in the diagram) also ranges in the 20s. The *tawa* has the shortest range in the late 20s.

The height of the lid and that of the *tawa* ranges below 10 cm. as also that of the cake bowl. But its median lies a little above the two former shapes. For the frying pan the height ranges in the middle 10s but its kurtosis dips below 10 cm.

The *tawa* leads in the opening range 130°–140°. It is followed by the lid ranging between 130°–110° but kurtosis goes down to 80s. The frying pan is more standardized ranging between 100°–110° or little over. The cake bowl is somewhat similar with kurtosis stretching to 90° and 120°.

The frying pan is a cooking vessel for deep frying or stir frying. Therefore, these vessels require less depth than boiling vessels but are less

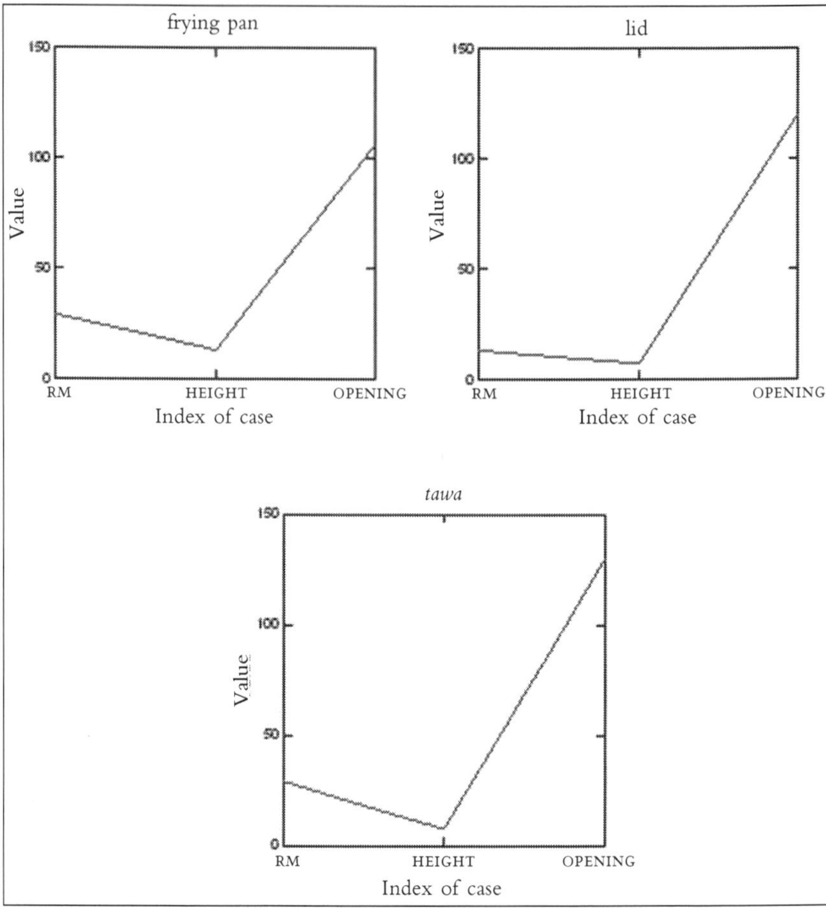

FIGURE 3.17: Dimensions of shallow open mouthed vessel

shallow than lid or *tawa*. The latter two have very little difference except range of size. Here proportion between the rim diameter and the height is the deciding factor. However large lid and *tawa* might appear the same as the slope between rim and height would be steeper (Fig. 3.17) because the height of both these shapes stay stable and does not increase with the increase in size.

Comparison between different *handis*

The slope between rim and the neck is gradual for beef and vegetable pot and almost flat for rice pot and *handi*. The slope from neck to body is similar in all the four cases. The slope from body to height is the steepest for vegetable pot and the dip is the least for beef pot. A similar contrast is visible in case of opening also. The variation between rice pot and *handi* is the least.

The rim diameters of beef cooking pots are the largest, ranging around 30 cm. Rice pot is the smallest ranging from below 20 to 25 cm. though the kurtosis of distribution stretch to below 15 cm. and above 30 cm. *Handi* (multipurpose) ranges between 20 and 30 cm. with kurtosis reaching below 20 cm. and above 30 cm. The rim diameter of the vegetable pot falls between that of the beef pot and rice pot.

Rice pots have the smallest neck and the diameter varies from mid 10s to early 20s. For the beef pots the size of neck is the most standardized of this group. *Handis* range between mid 10s to mid 20s with kurtosis stretching it to almost 40. The slope between the rim and neck (Fig. 3.18) is maximum in the case of vegetable pot.

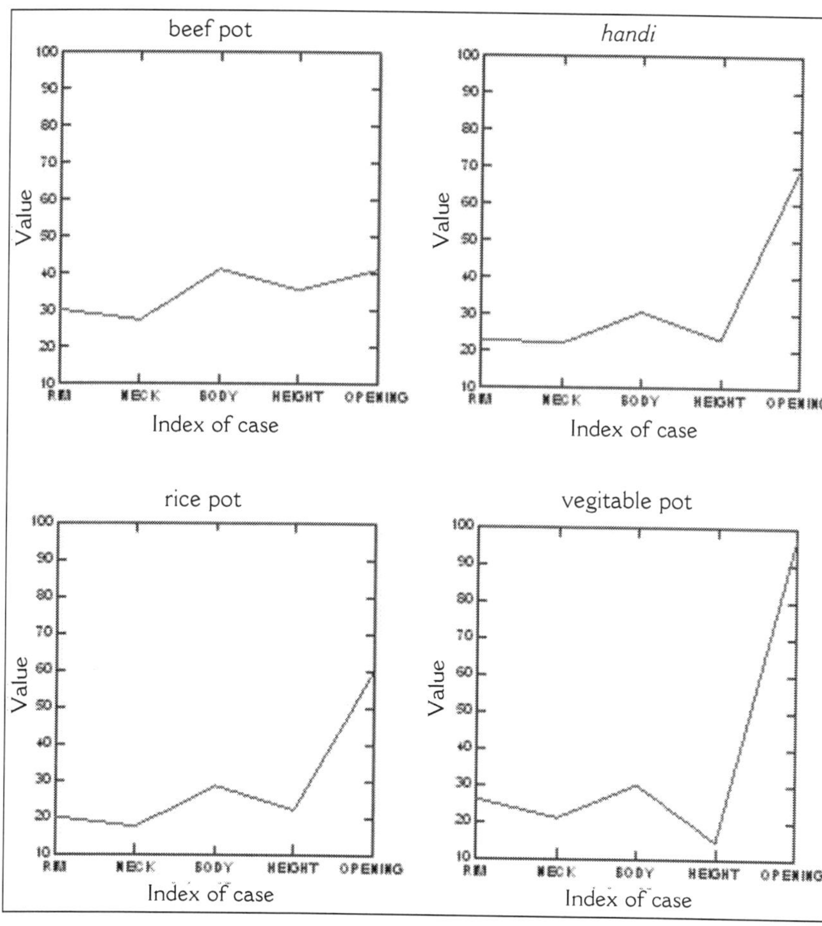

FIGURE 3.18: Dimensions of *handis*

The body of beef pots is the largest, mostly measuring above 40 cm. *Handis* range between late 20s and mid 30s with kurtosis stretching it down below 20 cm. The diameters of rice pots range between mid 20s to early 30s with kurtosis stretching to 20 cm. and almost to 40 cm. as also the case with vegetable pot.

Again beef pot is the tallest ranging between 20s and 40s. The height of rice pot is in 20s with a long kurtosis. *Handis* are similar to the rice pots. The height of the vegetable pot is the least, ranging 10–20 cm.

The opening of the beef pot measures from 34° to below 60° and the kurtosis stretches to 70°. That of the rice pot range between 50°–60° with kurtosis stretching to 40° and 70°. *Handis* have the larger opening of around 70° with kurtosis stretching beyond 80°. But for vegetable pot the median is at 95° and the largest is about 110°.

Beef pot need to be larger to cook meat for longer and in a lot more water. Therefore, it is the larger vessel. However, cooking beef needs better access to the interior than rice as the contents need to be stirred. *Handis*, because of their multipurpose use, have an average proportion and a larger opening than rice pots for similar reason but do not have the depth of beef pots. The opening of vegetable pot is the largest as it requires shallow frying together with boiling.

Beef pot is a large vessel and distinctly high. But the proportion of rim, neck and body diameters is same as rice *handi*. Proportion of rim to neck diameters is almost equal in case of multipurpose handi. The height of vegetable pot is the least.

Comparison between frying and roasting vessel

The rim diameter of frying pan (Fig. 3.17) is standardized and ranges between 20 and 30 cm. Roasters (Fig. 3.16) are larger, most of them varying between 40 and 60 cm., but kurtosis stretches to 90 cm. and 30 cm.

The height of the frying pan ranges under 10 cm. to mid 10s. The roaster ranges from the mid 10s to early 20s.

The opening of the frying pan is 100°–110°, with kurtosis stretching a little beyond. The *muri* roaster stretches between 90° and 110° with kurtosis stretching to 80° and 120°. *Muri* roasting involves large volume of grain and thereby requiring greater depth as well as larger diameter.

The foregoing discussion of morphometry of individual vessel types and the comparison with similar types shows that function is an important variable of variations in form.

Most of these vessels are available in a range of sizes depending on different consumption requirements. Most prominent are the frying pan and *muri* roaster, used for commercial and domestic purposes. It is also interesting to note that there is a general standard range for most household utensils.

We have also found in the previous section that in different vessels different components respond differently to variation. In that case, it might be better to seek a pattern of relationship as created by multivariate coordinated display (figures in this section) and assign them a functional name or group. Subjecting archaeological samples to this kind of analysis in complex cultures might give good results.

Regional variation in the pots

To see the regional variation of morphometry of different types of pots, a box plot of different parts were made. This would give an adequate reflection of variations noticed across the surveyed region.

Frying Pan: The median of rim diameter of all the districts is located near the 30 cm. mark. Bardhaman has some cases above as well as below this. In Birbhum, rim diameters of the frying pan are just under 30 cm., and those in South 24 Parganas fall a little below that mark. Pans from Malda have an upper hinge at 35 cm. but the height of those from the South 24 Parganas

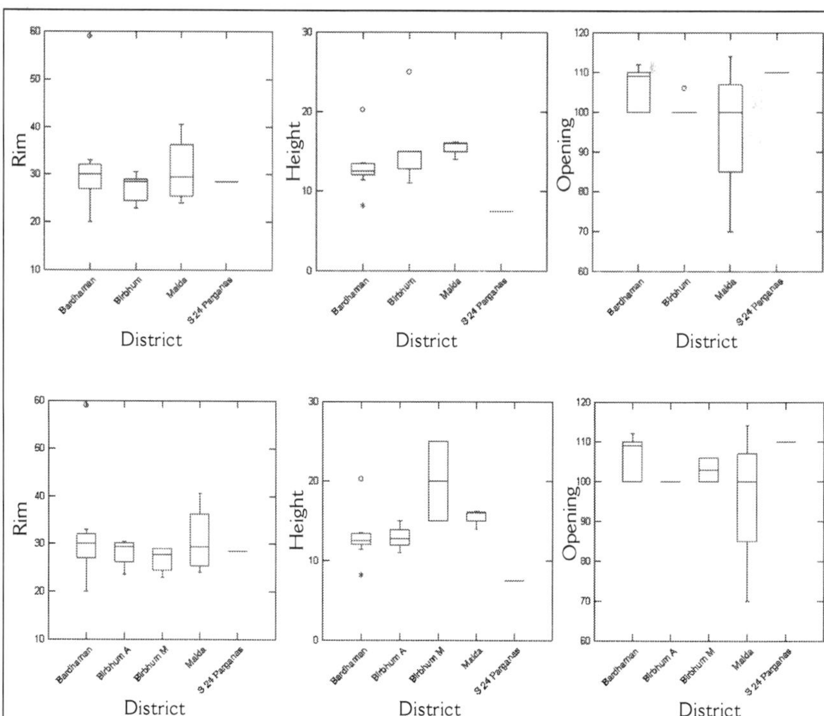

FIGURE 3.19: Box plots of frying pans from different districts

is quite shallow, under 10 cm. This is followed by the examples from Bardhaman and Birbhum. The samples from Malda, ranging in mid 10s, are the highest. However, villages on Mayurakshi in Birbhum have greater height (Fig. 3.19: Birbhum), mid 10s to mid 20s, than both Malda and average height of Birbhum. In these districts the opening angle of the vessel ranges between 100°–110°, but Malda ranges are 70°–110°. It is clear that frying pans of Malda are bigger than the rest.

Handi: The rim diameter in Bardhaman ranges between 20 cm. and over 25 cm. The vessels from Malda also have a wide range, from below 20 cm. to above 25 cm. In Birbhum we have the largest rim diameters, ranging from 25 cm. to 40 cm. Neck dimensions also follow a similar pattern. Body diamters of *handis* from Bardhaman ranges between 20 and 40 cm., in Malda it ranges from under 20 to mid 20s, and in Birbhum from under 30 to 50 cm. The height of specimens from Malda is only in mid 10s. The samples from Bardhaman range between 20 and 30 cm. and Birbhum from under 20 cm. to over 30 cm. The opening of the *handis* from Bardhaman and Birbhum are similar: 60°–70° and Malda is between 70°–80°. Birbhum *handis* tend to be of larger size and have a wider range, while Malda is shallower than the rest.

Muri roaster: South 24 Parganas is not represented. The rim diameter in Bardhaman is around 60 cm., Birbhum has a wider range from a little over 60 cm. to below 50 cm., while the rim diameter in Malda is much smaller,

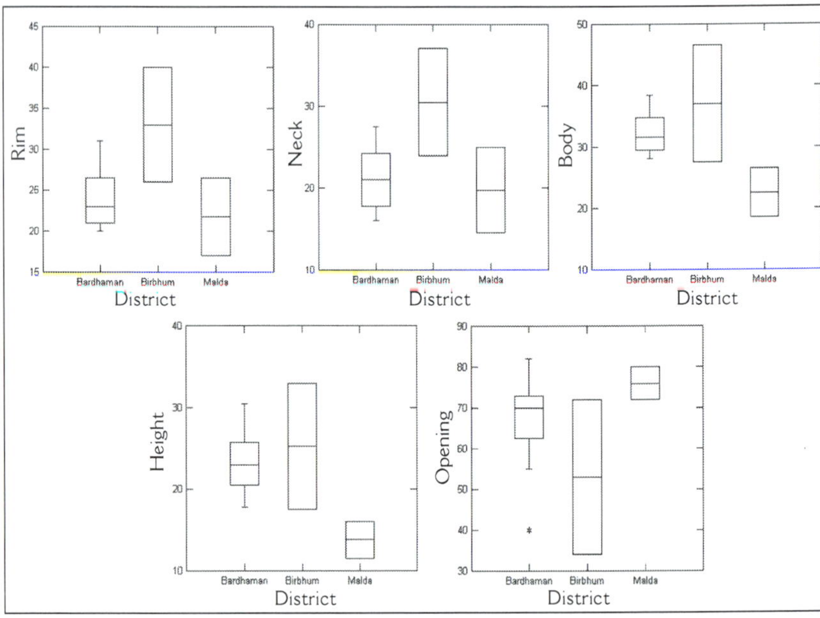

FIGURE 3.20: Box plots of *handi*s from different districts

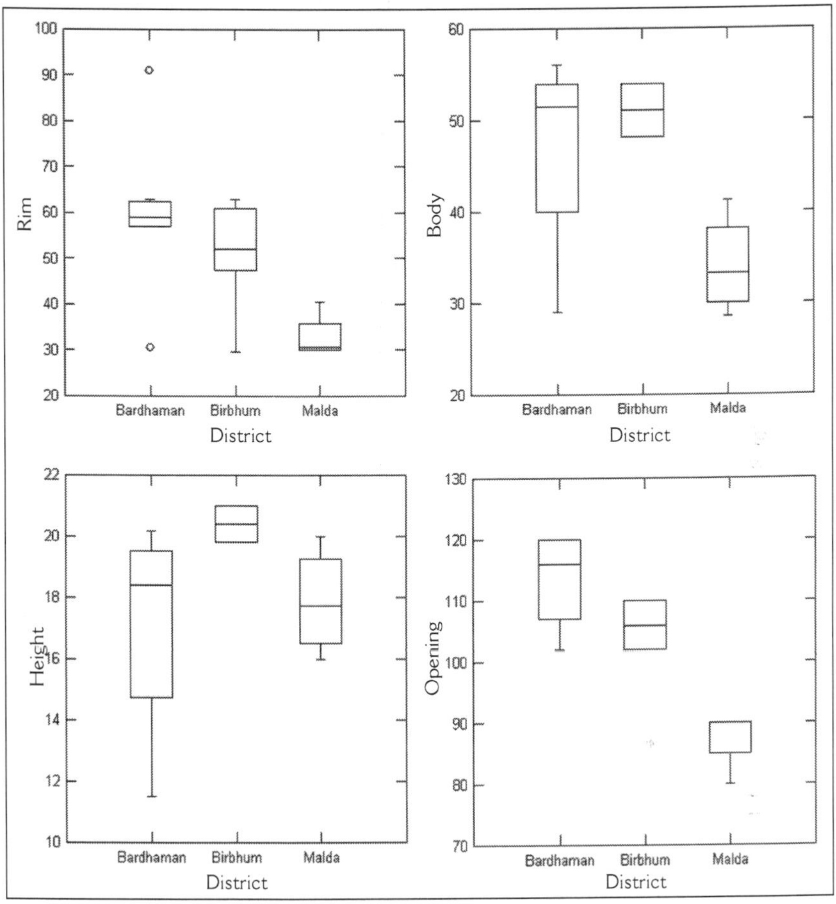

FIGURE 3.21: Box plots of *muri* roasters from different districts

30–40 cm. Body size from Bardhaman has a wider range, 30–50 cm. Those of Birbhum are standardized to mid 50s and the specimens from Malda range between 30 and 40 cm. The height of *muri* roasters from Birbhum is a standard 21 cm., those from Malda range between 16 and 20 cm., and in Bardhaman the height is between 12 and 21 cm. The openness of the mouth of roaster is the largest in Bardhaman ranging from 120° to 100°; in Birbhum it is between 110° and 100°; in Malda the opening is much smaller around 90°.

Muri Sieve: The median of rim diameter for all the three districts lies near 30 cm. While sizes found in Bardhaman and Birbhum are very standardized, Malda has a wide range, 40 cm. to less than 20 cm. The body diameters again show uniformity in Bardhaman and Birbhum, the former being slightly larger. In Malda the body size ranges between 20 and

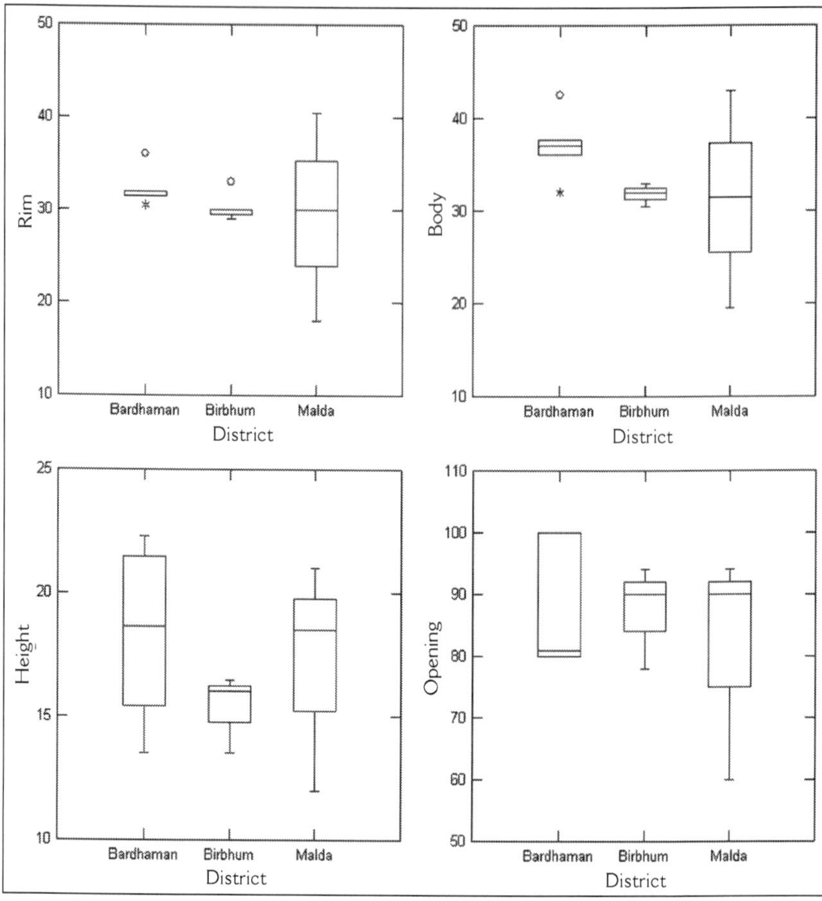

FIGURE 3.22: Box plots of *muri* sieves from different districts

45 cm. The box plot of Birbhum shows a standard height of around 15 cm. Bardhaman and Malda have *muri* sieve heights ranging from under 15 to 20 cm. Opening of the sieve in Birbhum is around 90°. In Bardhaman, the opening angle ranges between 80° and 100° with median close to 80° and in Malda it is a little over 90° to 60° with the median at 90°.

Rice pot: The rim diameter of both Bardhaman and South 24 Parganas show a very short range of 22–23 cm. and 19–20 cm. respectively. In Birbhum the range is 25 cm. to almost 30 cm. Malda also has a similar range. Neck of the rice pot in Bardhaman do not vary proportionately with the variation of rim diameter. In South 24 Parganas they vary a little. Bardhaman, Malda and Birbhum have a long range in neck diameters, 17–28 cm., below 15–23 cm., and 15 cm. to a little over 25 cm. respectively. Body diameter in all the districts shows a lot of variation. Malda and Bardhaman vary the most, from about 20 cm. to over 35 cm. and 20 to 40 cm. respectively. The height of Malda pots varies the most, from 25 to almost 40 cm. The opening of the rice pots from Bardhaman ranges between 50° and 80°, in Birbhum the range is 40°–80° (those from Mayurakshi bank are between 50° and 65°), in Malda it is between 60° and 55° and in South 24 Parganas it is 60°–50°. A wide range of body and height is usually associated with different size categories but the rim does not change proportionately. South 24 Parganas rice pots show the most standard dimensions.

Ritual bowl: Rim diameter does not show much variation within the districts, but inter-district variation is marked. The diameter of the rim in Bardhaman is 20–25 cm., Birbhum 25–30 cm., Malda about 17–26 cm., and South 24 Parganas is 20 cm. Body diameter varies with Bardhaman at 20 cm. and South 24 Parganas 22–24 cm., Malda 18–27 cm. and Birbhum ranging 22–33 cm. The height of the cases from Bardhaman and Malda ranges from 11 to 14 cm., South 24 Parganas 9 to 14 cm., Birbhum being different from the rest at 16 to 20 cm. The openings of the ritual bowl found in all the districts are very similar. Bardhaman ranges from 80–85°, Birbhum 80–84°, South 24 Parganas ranges 80–82° and Malda 78–80°.

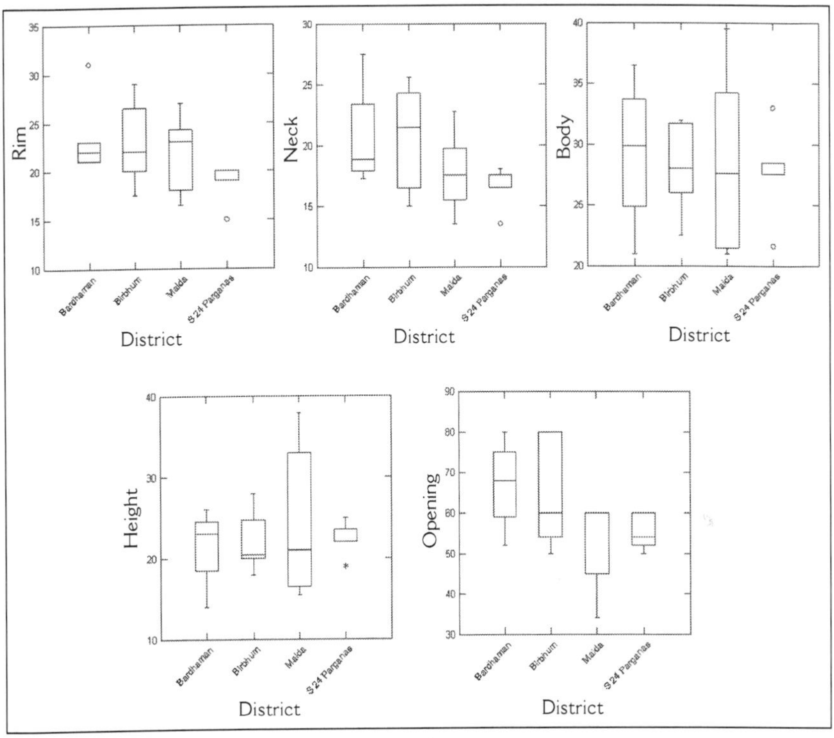

FIGURE 3.23: Box plots of rice pots from different districts

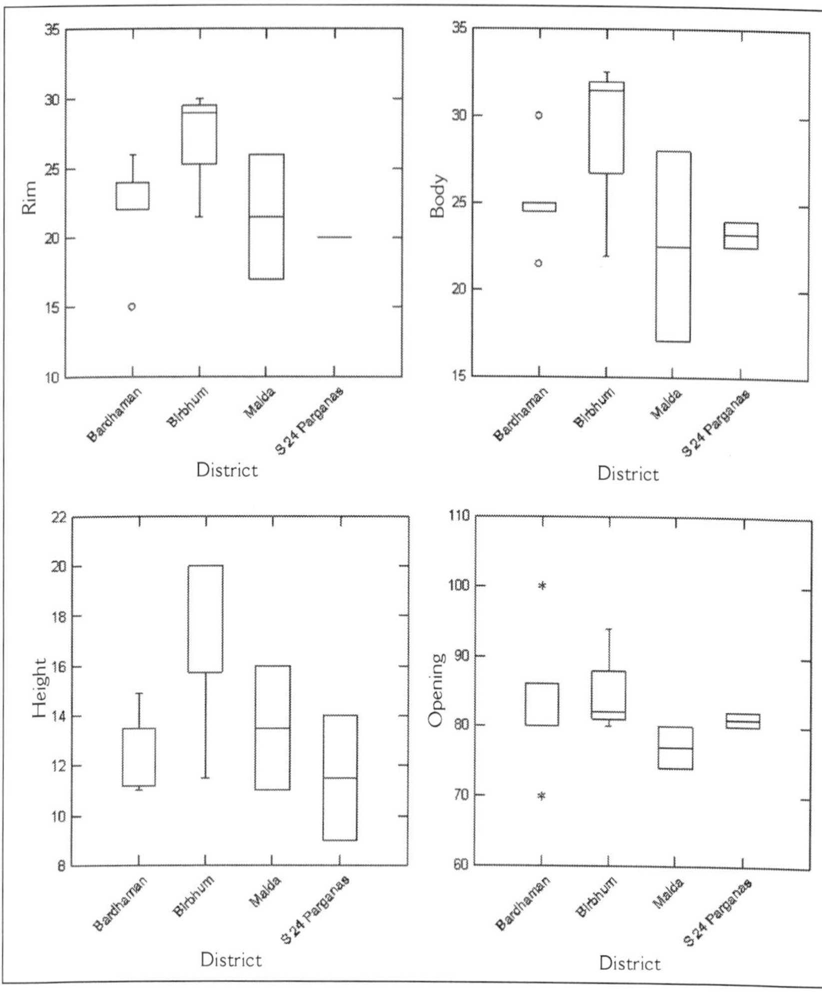

FIGURE 3.24: Box plots of ritual bowls from different districts

Ritual pot: The rim diameter of ritual pots shows a lot of variation in different regions as well as within each region. This is probably because ritual functions are different. At Bardhaman the rim diameter ranges between 13 and 18 cm., Birbhum 11and 14 cm., Malda 7 and 11 cm. and South 24 Parganas 12 and 14 cm. The size of the neck in this respect shows a lot of similarity, with the median hovering around 10 cm. except in Malda. Body diameter is also different. Bardhaman ranges between 20 and 30 cm., Birbhum 15 and 18 cm., Malda 15 and 8 cm., and South 24 Parganas 15 and 16 cm. In South 24 Parganas the height ranges from 15 to 25 cm. In Birbhum the upper limit of height is below 20 cm., and in Malda between 10 and 13 cm. The openings of ritual pots shows a more general pattern with median of all these regions near 40° and upper limit is 50°. The villages on the river Ajay in Birbhum district are roughly similar to that of Malda except the opening. However, importance of proportion in this shape is emphasized through similar pattern of box plots for all districts. The opening shows a reverse of the other patterns as it is inversely related to height.

Basin: In Bardhaman and Birbhum rim diameters are close, ranging from 45 to a little over 50 cm. and 40–50 cm. respectively. The rim diameter in Malda ranges from 50 cm. to a little over 60 cm. and those of South 24 Parganas are most varied with a range of 25–80 cm. The height of the basins at Malda and Birbhum are most uniform: 30 cm. and 41 cm respectively. In Bardhaman the height varies around 30–40 cm. with kurtosis going up to late 40s. South 24 Parganas range from 39–45 cm. with kurtosis going down to the early 30s. Opening is usually round; 80°–90° for Bardhaman and South 24 Parganas, though in the latter district it decreases to 70°. In Bibhum it is round 80° and in Malda, 90°–100°.

Vegetable pot: Malda has only one case and it represents a much larger vessel than the rest. The rims of Birbhum and South 24 Parganas

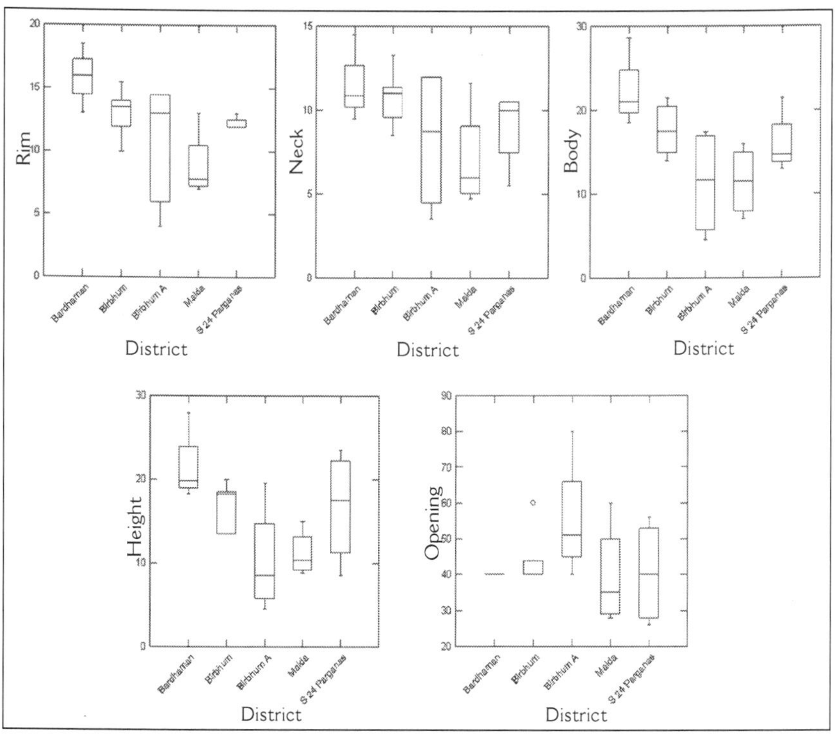

FIGURE 3.25: Box plots of ritual pots from different districts

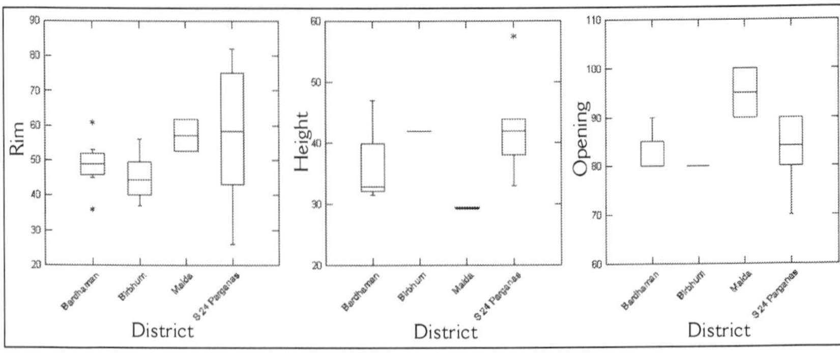

FIGURE 3.26: Box plot of basin from different districts

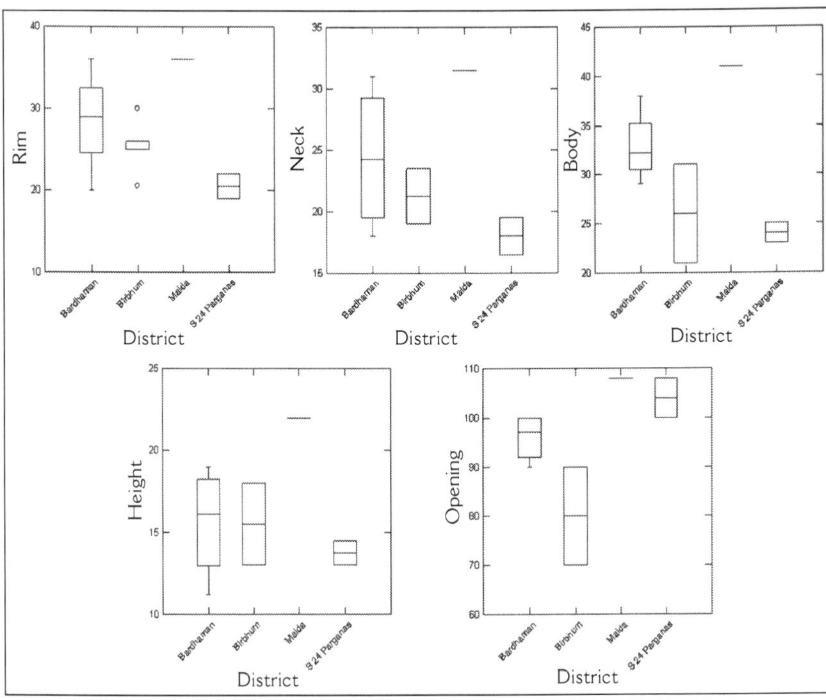

FIGURE 3.27: Box plot of vegetable pot from different districts

are standardized ranging between 20 cm. and 25 cm. In Bardhaman the size ranges around 25–30 cm. In South 24 Parganas the size of the body ranges between 24–25 cm., in Birbhum 20–30 cm. and in Bardhaman around 29–33 cm. The height of these pots from South 24 Parganas is around 13–15 cm., in Bardhaman 12–18 cm., and in Birbhum 13–17 cm. The opening of the vegetable pot in South 24 Parganas is 100°–110°, in Bardhaman it is 90°–100° and Birbhum it is 70°–90°. The vessels from South 24 Parganas are the smallest, but with a larger opening.

Water pitcher: There is in general very little variation in rim diameter. In Bardhaman the range is within 15–16 cm., in Birbhum it is 14.5–16 cm., in South 24 Parganas it is 13–15 cm. and in Malda the range is 12–16 cm. The variation in the neck diameter more or less corresponds to the variation in the rim diameter in all the districts. In Bardhaman and South 24 Parganas the range is 10–11 cm. and 11–12 cm. respectively, in Birbhum it is 9–13 cm. and in Malda it is about 6–10 cm. The cases from Bardhaman again have standard body diameters ranging 30–33 cm. but this is not true for other regions. Birbhum ranges from 23 to 37 cm., Malda 22–39 cm. and South 24 Parganas about 24–32 cm. Bardhaman again shows a lot of uniformity in height which is around 34 or 35 cm. In Birbhum the height ranges between 25 and 30 cm., Malda 25 and 40 cm., and South 24 Parganas early 20s to just below 40 cm. The pitchers from the Ajay valley, in Birbhum, show greater uniformity but are closer to those from Mayurakshi valley than Bardhaman. The opening of a pitcher is always narrow. In South 24 Parganas the range is 20°–30° and in Malda around 20°, as also for Bardhaman and Birbhum, 25°–30°. Since none of the villages are far from water source, Birbhum, with less constricted necks and over all smaller sizes of water pitchers, shows a slightly different pattern.

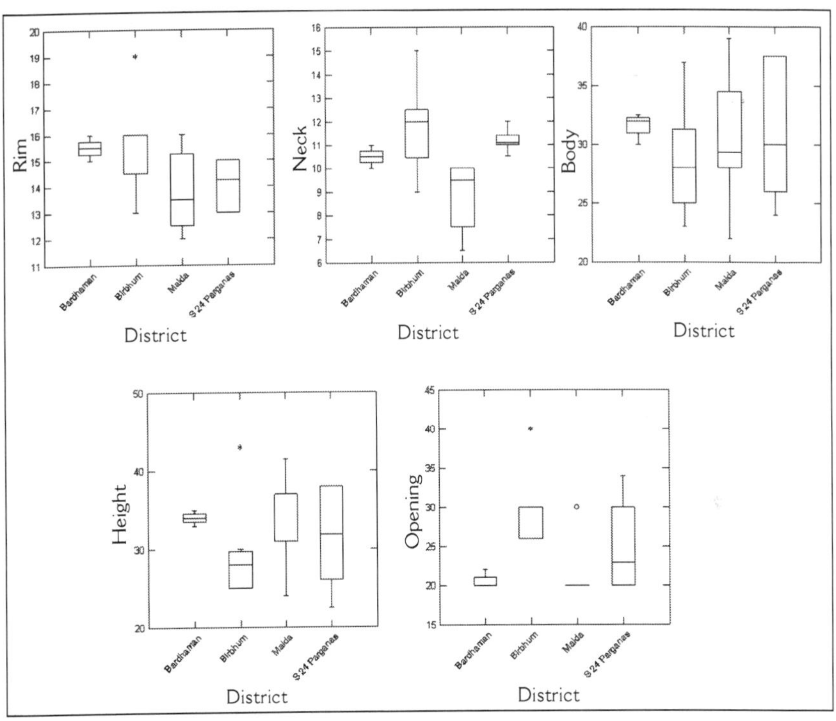

FIGURE 3.28: Box plots of water pitchers from different districts

DISCUSSION

The forgoing sections show that the vessels can be roughly divided into two groups, those displaying proportionate change and those that change disproportionately. The first group includes *handi*, sieve, ritual bowl, ritual pot and vegetable pot. The second group includes the frying pan, roaster, basin, rice pot and water pitcher. In the first group the size of every portion increases and decreases with the general size of the vessel and this is true in different districts as function dictates that proportions have to be maintained for all parts. In fact, for the *handi* (including all the variants) a small change in proportion is associated with different functions. The range of size available in a region is according to the need of the inhabitants.

In the second group, sizes do not change proportionately. The functions of these vessels are again responsible for this. The emphasis is on just two aspects for the frying pan and roaster—height and opening. For the pitcher a change in size can only be achieved through body and height. The rice pot maintains proportion between neck and rim but the body or height does not change in similar proportion. The change in the size of the vessel in this case too is reflected in the proportion of body and height, but a change in rim and neck size may or may not take place. Basin being a multipurpose vessel is more flexible.

The sizes of the vessels of different types do not suggest any regional patterning. There is a general uniformity among types from different regions. Variations recorded in the range of sizes could be partly due to the availability of these different sizes. However, some sizes are associated with local ways of use. For example *muri* roaster of Malda is of same size as the sieve. Here the sieve is placed on top of the roaster so that the sand gets back into the latter vessel. The sieves of Bardhaman and Birbhum are without perforation and the sand is allowed to settle down. Basins from Bardhaman and Birbhum are essentially to feed cows, so sizes do not vary too much. In South 24 Parganas it is also used to store paddy temporarily or to soak paddy before boiling it for processing rice, and these are found in multiple sizes.

TRANS-REGION VARIATION OF FORMS

It can be gleaned from the earlier discussion that a range of utility ware is produced and consumed. There are several types which are universally found with some variations. I have referred above to a general similarity in size over a region and in many cases this is even found throughout the surveyed area. If we look at form there is also an apparent similarity. But there are also intra- and inter-regional differences.

TABLE 3.1: Pitchers and their constituent parts

Village	*Rim form*	*Neck shape*	*Body shape*	*Base*
Krishnapalli (Malda)	Flaring externally thickened triangular	Tapering	Bulging	Round
Kadubari (Malda) 1	Horizontally splayed	Concave	Bulging	Round
Kadubari (Malda) 2	Outturned clubbed straight	Concave	Bulging	Round
Kadubari (Malda) 3	Flaring clubbed rounded	Concave	Bulging	Round
Shikharbali (S. 24 Parganas)	Flaring externally thick rounded	Tapering	Bulging	Round
Shikarbali (S. 24 Parganas)	Outturned clubbed square	Short concave	Bulging	Round
Mondalpara (S. 24 Parganas)	Outturned clubbed concave	Short concave	Bulging	Round
Gorerhat (S. 24 Parganas)	Flaring externally thick rounded rim	Concave	Bulging	Round
Tatipara (S. 24 Parganas)	Flaring externally thick triangular	Concave	Bulging	Round
Gabberia (S. 24 Parganas	Flaring clubbed straight	Short concave	Bulging	Round
Jalpara (Bardhaman)	Flaring clubbed square	Tapering	Bulging	Round
Ichchhabat (Bardhaman)	Flaring externally thick triangular with ridged top	Concave	Bulging	Round
Gafulia (Bardhaman)	Flaring externally thick triangular	Short concave	Globular	Round
Mahula (Birbhum)	Outturned clubbed	Tapering	Bulging	Round
Nastika (Birbhum)	Flaring externally thick triangular	Concave	Bulging	Round
Ramkrishnapur (Birbhum)	Flaring clubbed everted	Tapering	Bulging	Round
Shyamnona (Birbhum)	Outturned clubbed triangular	Tapering	Bulging	Round

Gafulia, Bardhaman | Boyargadi, South 24 Parganas | Kadubari, Malda

PLATE 3.1: Water pitchers of different shapes

TABLE 3.2: Water jars and their constituent parts

Village	*Rim form*	*Neck shape*	*Body shape*	*Base*
Batashpur (Birbhum)	Outturned clubbed	Short concave	Globular	Round
Nastika (Birbhum)	Flaring externally thickened sloping	Short tapering	Bulging	Round
Shyamnona (Birbhum)	Outturned clubbed with bisecting groove	Short concave	Bulging	Round
Shyamnona (Birbhum)	Flaring externally sloping	Constricted	Rounded	Round
Kashinarar (S. 24 Parganas)	Outturned clubbed triangular	Short concave	Rounded	Round
Gabberia (S. 24 Parganas)	Outturned externally thickened rim	Concave	Globular	Round
Bonpara (Bardhaman)	Flaring externally sloping	Constricted	Globular	Round
Ichchhabat (Bardhaman)	Splayed everted	Constricted	Globular	Round
Khajurdihi (Bardhaman)	Flaring externally sloping	Constricted	Bulging	Round

The shapes of water pitcher (*kalsi*) are broadly similar with some variation at the rim. The shape of a pitcher allows water to be filled and restricts spillage. For Malda the constriction of the neck is more acute. In a similar way shortened neck of one type from Shikharbali with clubbed rim makes it a distinct type.

The water jars have short necks in comparison to pitchers. The overall size could be larger than a pitcher but some are smaller, the body is most times rounded but can also be elongated.

There are some other storage vessels for liquids such as wine, date juice and palm juice. These may look like water jar or pitcher (like date

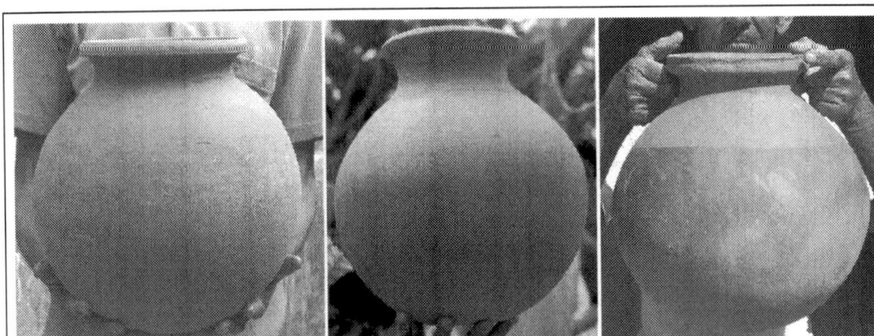

Batashpur (Birbhum) Gabbreia (South 24 Pargana) Shyamnona (Birbhum)

PLATE 3.2: Water jars of different shapes

TABLE 3.3: *Handis* and their constituent parts

Village	*Rim form*	*Neck shape*	*Body shape*	*Base*
Kadubari (Malda)	Thick splayed	Short concave	Bulging	Round
Krishnapalli (Malda)	Obliquely splayed	Constricted	Carinated waist	Round
Bonpara (Bardhaman)	Obliquely splayed	Constricted	Carinated waist	Round
Jalpara (Bardhaman)	Obliquely splayed	Constricted	Carinated waist	Round
Ichchhabat (Bardhaman)	Obliquely splayed externally thick	Constricted	Carinated waist	Round
Khejurdihi (Bardhaman)	Obliquely splayed externally sloping	Constricted	Bulging	Round
Gafulia (Bardhaman)	Horizontally splayed	Short concave	Sharply carinated waist	Round
Batashpur (Birbhum)	Thick obliquely splayed	Constricted	Carinated waist	Round
Bishaypur (Birbhum)	Horizontally splayed	Constricted	Carinated waist	Round

juice vessel from South 24 Parganas). However, they carry some small difference from the water vessel in their locality, thus marking a different utility to the consumer.

The pots which are used for tapping palmyra palm juice (tied to the top of the trunk where leaves brunch out of the trunk) are usually smaller. They may have a collared rim and flaring body, or splayed rim with constricted neck and bulging body, easy to hang on the tree. While the mouth of the date juice collector vessel is narrow so that the birds cannot drink from it, that of palmyra is larger to accommodate the area of seepage (according to the potters).

There are some other pots, I was told, manufactured without specific purpose in mind and used as containers. These usually have a simple shape with a slightly thickened and outturned rim, short, slightly constricted neck and rounded body—no part is emphasized.

In the villages of Bardhaman district *handis* show a broad similarity except those for cooking beef used by Muslims. There are also *handis* for

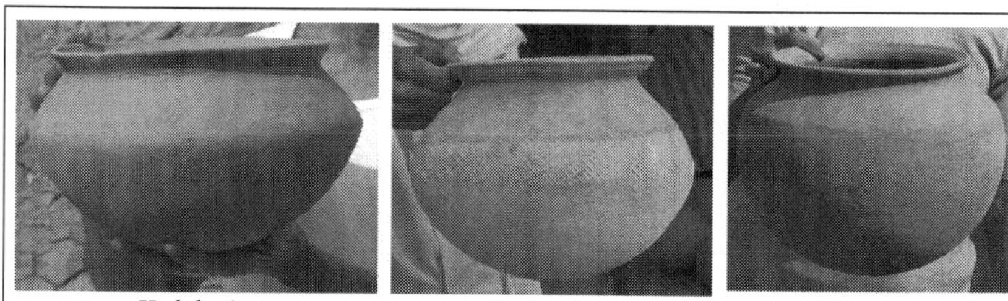

Kadubari Bishaypur Bonpara

PLATE 3.3: *Handis* of different shapes

TABLE 3.4: Rice pot and its constituent parts

Village	*Rim form*	*Neck shape*	*Body shape*	*Base*
Kadubari (Malda) 1	Obliquely splayed	Constricted	Flaring, bulge lower down	Round
Kadubari (Malda) 2	Horizontally splayed	Short concave	Globular	Round
Krishnapalli (Malda)	Horizontally splayed	Short concave	Bulging	Round
Phulbaria (Malda)	Horizontally splayed	Constricted	Bulging	Round
Nakali (S. 24 Pargana)	Obliquely splayed	Constricted	Carinated waist	Round
Shikarbali (S. 24 Pargana)	Thick splayed	Constricted	Carinated middle	Round
Bishaypur (Birbhum)	Short obliquely splayed	Constricted	Carinated waist	Round
Mahula (Birbhum	Obliquely splayed	Constricted	Carinated waist	Round
Ramkrishnapur (Birbhum) 1	Thick obliquely splayed	Short tapering	Carinated waist	Round
Ramkrishnapur (Birbhum) 2	Flaring clubbed	Short concave	Carinated waist	Round
Thupsara (Birbhum	Flaring externally thickened	Constricted	Bulging	Round
Shyamnona (Birbhum)	Obliquely splayed	Constricted	Carinated shoulder	Round
Bonpara (Bardhaman)	Obliquely splayed	Constricted	Bulging	Round
Jalapara (Bardhaman) 1	Obliquely splayed	Constricted	Bulging	Round
Jalapara (Bardhaman) 2	Thick obliquely splayed	Constricted neck	Globular	Round
Gafulia (Bardhaman)	Short splayed	Short concave	Bulging	Round

boiling/soaking paddy. A few variations were also noticed in Birbhum district, which are related to its use. Malda *handis* are more open.

The *handi* for cooking rice forms a separate type with distinct varieties. While a closed mouthed vessel is used in South 24 Parganas and parts of Bardhaman, open mouthed vessels are favoured in Birbhum district.

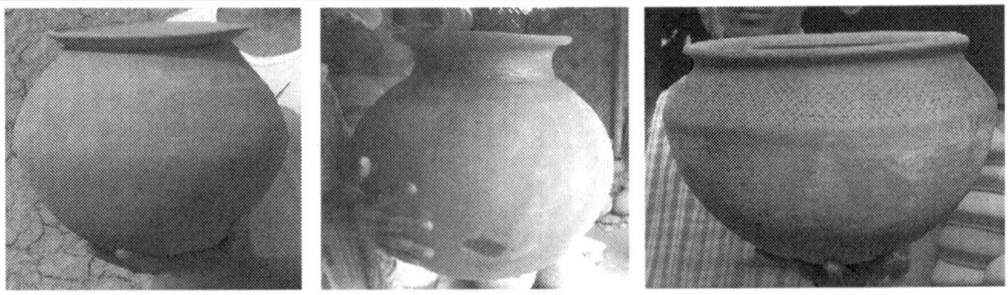

Bonpara, Bardhaman Kadubari, Malda Nastika, Birbhum

PLATE 3.4: Rice pots of different shapes

The *handi* from Malda is close mouthed. Compared to the other *handis*, the rice *handi* is usually deeper with a narrower mouth. Most of the shapes have splayed rims and constricted necks. While the body shapes of Malda and Bardhaman pots are bulging, those of Birbhum and South 24 Parganas are carinated. Kramer (1997), incidentally, noted that carination was a stylistic phenomena not related to manufacturing technique. The concave neck of Kadubari is distinctly different, but the short tapering neck at Ramkrishnapur is probably a manufacturing variation unlike the flaring clubbed rim which is deliberate (see page 132).

A smaller pot, alternatively referred to as *bhand* or *handi,* is made in Bardhaman and South 24 Parganas district respectively, for sweet shops. The shapes are more rounded and open in Barbhaman. The term *bhand* is used in South 24 Parganas and Kolkata for vessels which are more open mouthed and usually have a flat base. A smaller variety is used for selling tea. The *bhand* is entirely manufactured on the wheel, more suitable for mass production and caters to large markets.

The storage jars of South 24 Parganas are usually large with externally thickened or collared (more popular) rim and with an oblong to tapering body. These are for storing water and used by small eateries and sweet shops. A smaller version is made for domestic use. These may have a collared, externally drooping or externally thickened rim.

At Thupsara (Birbhum) a similar large jar with flaring rim and globular body is used for soaking paddy. Basin is used in South 24 Parganas and Medinipur district to soak paddy. These are with large mouth and collared or splayed rim.

TABLE 3.5: *Muri* Roaster and its constituent parts

Village	*Rim form*	*Neck shape*	*Body shape*	*Base*
Ichchhabat (Bardhaman)	Outcurved thick drooping	None	Convex	Round
Gafulia (Bardhaman)	Outcurved thick drooping	None	Convex	Round
Jalpara (Bardhaman)	Outcurved thick drooping	None	Convex	Round
Banpara (Bardhaman)	Outcurved thick drooping	None	Convex	Round
Mahula (Birbhum	Outcurved thick drooping	None	Convex	Round
Nastika (Birbhum)	Short obliquely splayed	Constricted	Carinated waist	Round
Kadubari (Malda)	Short obliquely splayed	Constricted	Carinated waist	Round
Krishnapalli (Malda)	Obliquely splayed externally thickened	Constricted	Bulging	Round
Mathurapur (Malda)	Horizontally splayed	Constricted	Mildly carinated waist	Round
Phulbari (Malda)	Obliquely splayed rim	Constricted	Bulging	Round

Roasters for *muri* are also similar throughout Bardhaman and Birbhum. They have a convex body and splayed rim, except for Nastika in Birbhum, which is similar to the Malda variety. At Malda the roasters have splayed rims, constricted to short necks, and globular to bulging bodies.

PLATE 3.5: *Bonpara* roaster

The sieve for *muri* is the same in Bardhaman and Birbhum. It is a bowl shaped vessel, large and deep, with incurved rim from which a predestined part is deeply engraved and knocked off after firing. At Malda it is a perforated vessel of similar shape as the roaster.

PLATE 3.6: *Thupsara* sieve

The vessel for feeding cows (*patna or daba*) is the same in Bardhaman and Birbhum. The round bottom flaring sided pot stands on a support of mud encasement. In South 24 Parganas it is the basin which is used. But it is a multiple use vessel and broader base allows it to stand on its own. Sometimes it is a *mejla*, a less sturdy vessel with flaring rim and short height, is used to feed animals and is stuck in a mud encasement.

Gafulia, Bardhaman　　Gabberia, South 24 Parganas

PLATE 3.7: Basin of different shapes

The roaster (*chatu* or *tawa*) for *roti* is an innovation in a predominantly rice eating land. It is usually a large lid or else a form of *sara* (tray of offering). Some handled *chatu* is also made in South 24 Parganas. But in Malda the roasters used by Muslims are like a shallow open-mouthed *handis*. This, according to the potters, is because they eat thicker *roti*.

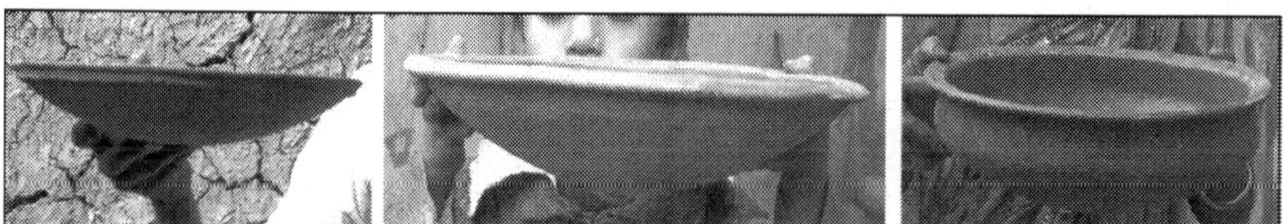

Bopara, Bardhaman　　Kadubari, Malda　　Mathurapur, Malda

PLATE 3.8: *Tawa* of different shapes

The looped handled pan is similar everywhere except at Gafulia (Bardhaman), which has externally thickened rim. This type is also found at Kadubari (Malda). The pan is always mould-made as it would be faster and easier.

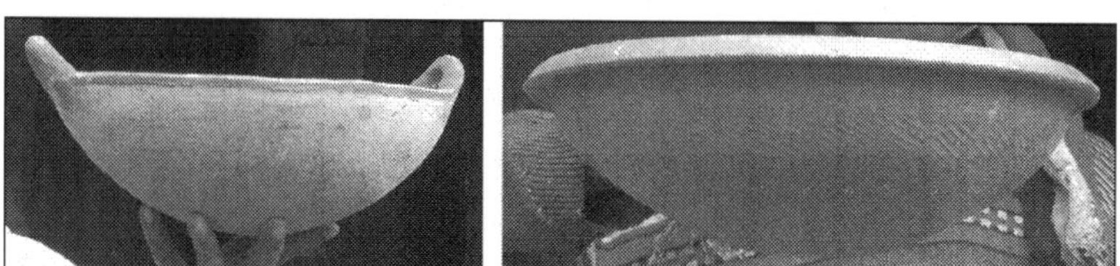

Ichchhabat, Bardhaman　　Kejurdihi, Bardhaman

PLATE 3.9: Frying pans of different shapes

The handless frying pan which was seen only in Birbhum and Bardhaman has thick externally sloping rim or collared rim in most cases except in Shyamnona and Mahula of Birbhum, which has outcurved internally thickened rim.

There is another group of cooking vessels (*tijel*), sometimes referred to as *kadai* but are less open. They are found in Bardhaman, for cooking vegetables and occasionally for boiling milk. There is a thickened flaring rim and biconical body. It is mostly found in Bardhaman but also noticed in Birbhum and South 24 Parganas.

Gafulia, Bardhaman

PLATE 3.10: *Tijel*

The greatest amount of variations are found in the case of ritual pots. The rim varies from externally thickened, clubbed to featureless. The neck is concave to constricted and the base could be flat or rounded. The body is usually well rounded and often decorated. These variations have very little relation to the geography. The size variation is usually related

Mahula, Bardhaman

Tantirhat South 24 Parganas

Nastika, Birbhum

Gabberia, South 24 Parganas

PLATE 3.11: Ritual pots of different shapes

to the type of ritual the pot is associated with. Against this variation of shape one should note the uniformity displayed in morphometry. This is essentially because all the pots are open-mouthed, with narrow neck and bulging body. Though they are ritual specific, they, most often, contain water and symbolize fertility and prosperity.

In contrast, the bowl for ritual food (*malsa*) shows homogeneity over a large area. It is a bowl with closing (inturned to make it parallel to base) rim. On most occasions it is handmade or otherwise mould made. The shape is different in Kadubari (Malda), where it has an incurved collared rim. At Nastika (Birbhum), *malsa* is used for cooking and has a splayed short thickened rim and carinated body and very closely resembles the *handi*.

Kashinagar | Mahula

PLATE 3.12: *Malsa* or the ritual bowl

In sum, in the three zones there are regional similarities and variations in the types of vessels. There are a set of vessels which are common to all these regions. This is because of similarity in food habits. Within each region features are usually common. But in the west villages of two different districts exhibit some differences. The villages of Birbhum on the Ajay River are physically nearer Bardhaman and share more common features than those on Mayurakshi. The main market for these villages is to the north, Bolpur in Birbhum district. The villages in the Bardhaman district sell their pots mostly at Katwa, situated on the bank of Ajay River. Therefore, the similarity in the present-day pottery of the villages on the Ajay River, located in Bardhaman and Birbhum, must be attributed to the past when the waterway was an important means of communication.

When studying archaeological ceramics we rely on morphometry to determine functional type. This study shows that this approach is useful only in certain cases. Some shapes have similar proportions in all the districts like the lid, vegetable pot, etc. In some forms, like the rice pot or *muri* roaster, there may be similarity only between two districts. In the case of the water pitcher, body parts do not vary proportionately in relation to size. Within a locality varieties of the same form may be present. But some of the vessels like rice pot and *handi* show similarity of form throughout the area, albeit with minor variations.

4

Pots from the Local Market

TOGETHER WITH THE SURVEY, as described earlier, of the household-workshops of the potters in different regions, another survey was conducted in *hats* or local markets where the finished products are sold. We can see from the earlier discussion that pottery production in South 24 Parganas has revealed the height level of standardization among the twenty-seven villages covered in the survey. That is why a market from this area was selected to see what kind of variations could be noticed in a local market from which most of the users would buy. There are several markets in this region. Raydighi and Kashinagar are the most prominent. The Raydighi market is larger and it caters to most of the villages located south of Jaynagar-Majilpur. But it has only two or three proper shops which sell pots. These are owned by traders not related to production. A few individual potters also would go there and sell their vessels from time to time in the open area. The shops procure pottery from Boyargadi and Kashinagar where they have fixed potters who supply them and also buy from traders who carry it across the river by boat from Ghatal in East Medinipur district.

Kashinagar Mai-Bibir *hat* was selected for survey as it has a dedicated lane within the market and consists of seven odd shops of different sizes selling pottery. The variety noticed here is much larger. These shops stock, individually, the pottery mostly made by a single household of potters, but supplement it in times of demand with pottery from others. The produce from nearby villages is sold together with items coming from Beral in East Medinipur district. Shops are sometimes owned by potters and sometimes by simple retailers but usually belonging to the potter community.

From a shop where different types of pottery are sold, five individual types of vessels of daily use were selected. It was ensured that each chosen type was from a single potter. Then some more types were also selected from different shops. Cross-sections of these pots were drawn to examine the exact difference in the shape. The emphasis was on the rims, especially for the large pots, because it is the most recorded feature in archaeological literature. Besides, it is difficult to break a pot in a way that reveals the entire cross-section. The purpose that would have served in any case is not clear. We know that even the wheel-made parts are not uniform, the lower parts of large pots, which are handmade (added to the shoulder and expanded by beating with a paddle and anvil), are likely to be uneven.

Description of Samples

PLATE 4.1: Dish

1. Dish (*thala*) [3]—handmade; external surface is slightly irregular; slipped internally and over the rim to fall down the outer surface, body height around 5 cm. The variants of this type are:

   (a) 24 cm. diameter, flaring sides, externally sloping rim, flat base.
   (b) 25 cm. diameter, flaring sides, externally sloping rim, flat base.
   (c) 27 cm. diameter, vertical sides, externally sloping rim, flat base.
   (d) 24 cm. diameter, outturned sides, externally sloping rim, flat base.
   (e) 25 cm. diameter, outturned sides, externally sloping rim, flat base.

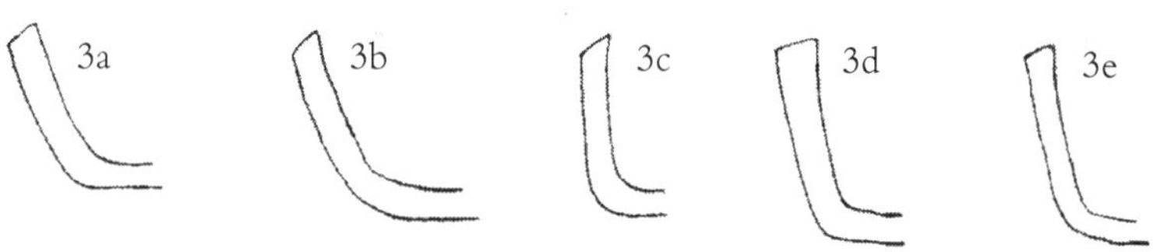

FIGURE 4.1: Section of dish

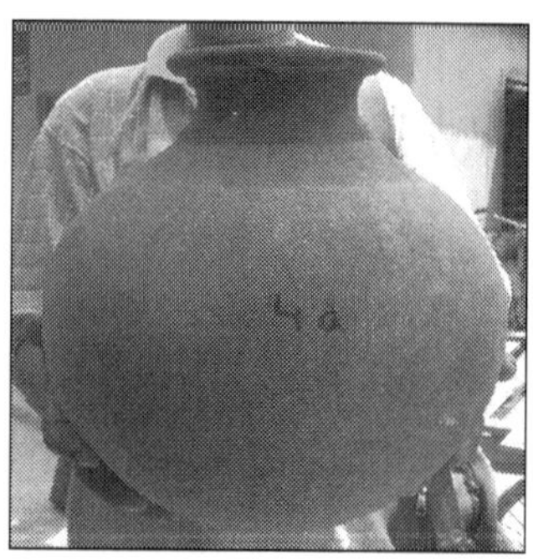

PLATE 4.2: Water pitcher

2. Water pitcher (*jaler kalashi*) [4]—wheel-made till half body, red slip on the rim and externally up to the shoulder, black painting on the neck, rounded body and base, height is 30 cm. The variations in this category are:

   (a) 12 cm. diameter, outturned, externally thickened and internally grooved rim, convave neck, sloping shoulder.
   (b) 13 cm. diameter, outturned, externally thickened and internally grooved rim, concave neck, sloping shoulder.
   (c) 13.2 cm. diameter, outturned, externally thickened and internally grooved rim, concave neck, sloping shoulder.
   (d) 13.4 cm. diameter, outturned, externally thickened and internally grooved rim, concave neck, sloping shoulder.
   (e) 13 cm. diameter, outturned, externally thickened and internally grooved rim, concave neck, rounded shoulder.

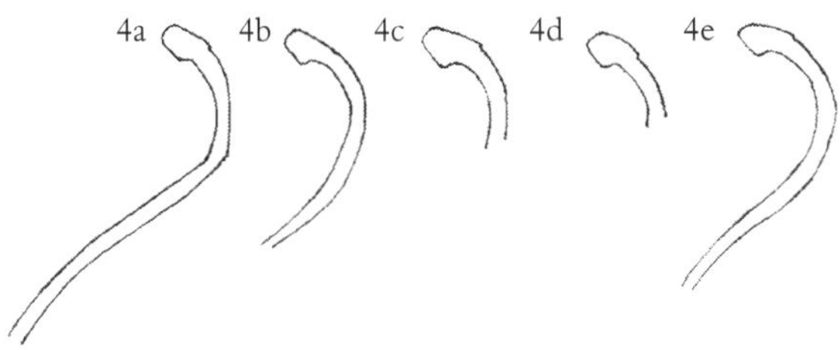

FIGURE 4.2: Section of water pitchers

PLATE 4.3: Date juice pitcher

3. Date juice pitcher [4]—rounded body and base, around 33 cm. height. Profiles vary as follows.

   (1a) 15 cm. diameter, splayed obliquely, clubbed square and internally sloping rim, concave neck, rounded shoulder.

(1b) 14 cm. diameter, splayed obliquely, clubbed rounded rim and internally grooved, concave neck, sloping shoulder.
(2a) 14 cm. diameter, splayed obliquely, clubbed rounded rim and internally grooved, concave neck, sloping shoulder.
(2b) 13 cm. diameter, flaring, clubbed rounded rim and internally grooved, concave neck sloping shoulder.

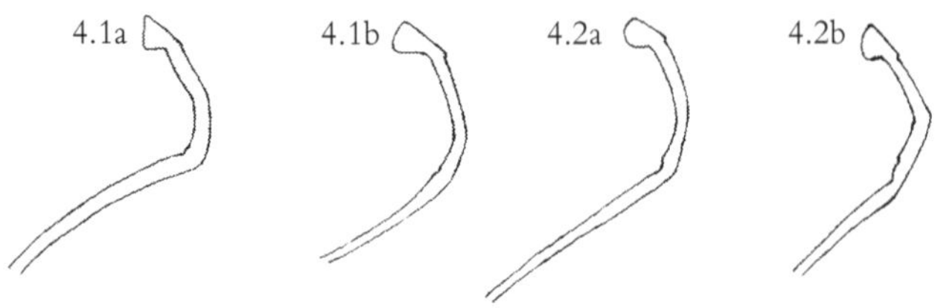

FIGURE 4.3: Section of date juice pitchers

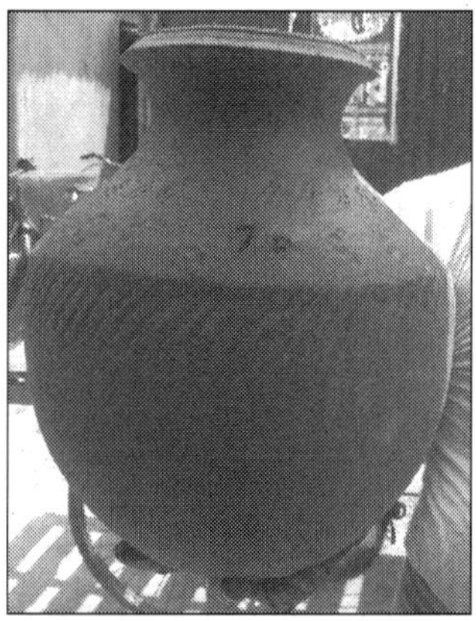

PLATE 4.4: Water jar

4. Water jar (*jaler dabar*) [7]—wheel-made to shoulder. The body is separately made and attached. Paddle impressions are visible a round the carination of shoulder. It is externally slipped till shoulder. The shoulder is also decorated with shallow groove and stamped design. The height is about 26 cm. This is a storage vessel unlike the pitcher which is meant for transport also. Variants are:

(a) 10.5 cm. diameter, outturned, externally thick triangular and slightly drooping rim with shallow groove and internal depression, concave neck, sloping shoulder.
(b) 10 cm. diameter, outturned, externally thick triangular rim with ridged top and internal depression, concave neck, sloping shoulder.

(c) 10 cm. diameter, outturned, externally thick triangular rim with ridged top and internal depression, concave neck, sloping shoulder.
(d) 10 cm. diameter, outturned, externally thick triangular rim with ridged top and internal depression, concave neck, sloping shoulder.
(e) 10 cm. diameter, outturned, externally thick triangular rim with ridged top and internal depression, tapering neck, sloping shoulder.

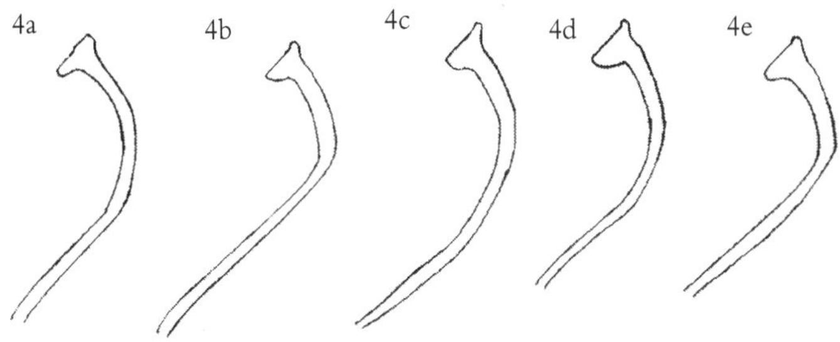

FIGURE 4.4: Section of water jars

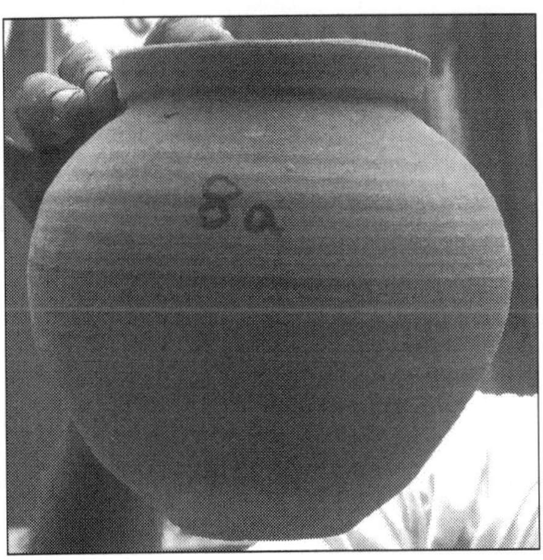

PLATE 4.5: Water pot

5. Water pot (*jaler bhand*) [8]—totally wheel-made, mild corrugation on body, flat base, about 14 cm. height. Examples are:

(a) 9.5 cm. diameter, flaring collared rim with internal depression, constricted neck, rounded shoulder, bulging body.
b) 10 cm. diameter, flaring collared rim with internal depression, constricted neck, rounded shoulder, bulging corrugated body.

(c) 10 cm. diameter, flaring collared concave rim with internal depression, constricted neck, rounded shoulder, bulging body.
(d) 9.5 cm. diameter, flaring collared concave rim internal depression rim, constricted neck, rounded shoulder, rounded body.
(e) 10 cm. diameter, flaring collared concave rim with internal depression, constricted neck, rounded shoulder, rounded corrugated body.

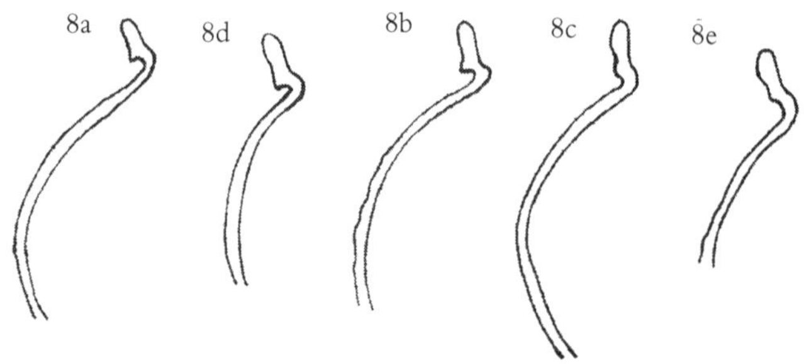

FIGURE 4.5: Section of water pots

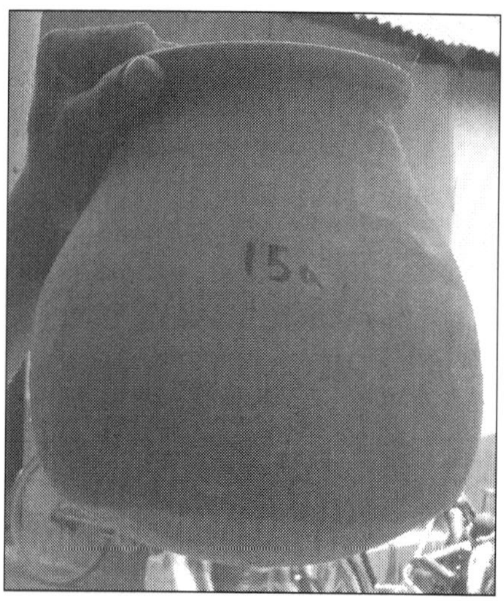

PLATE 4.6: Pot for collecting date juice

6. Pot for collecting date juice (*raser bhand*) [15]—partly wheel-made, flaring body, 22 cm. height. Profiles vary as follows.

   (a) 12.5 cm. diameter, flaring, externally thickened and undercut rim, concave neck, sloping ridged shoulder.
   (b) 13 cm. diameter, flaring, externally thickened and straightened rim, concave neck, sloping shoulder.

(c) 13 cm. diameter, flaring, externally thickened and rounded rim, concave neck, sloping shoulder.
(d) 13 cm. diameter, flaring externally thickened and straightened rim, concave neck, sloping ridged shoulder.
(e) 11.5 cm. diameter, flaring clubbed rim, constricted neck, sloping ridged shoulder.

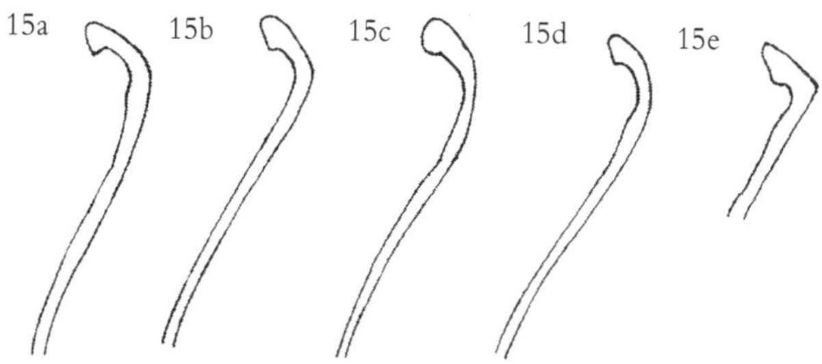

FIGURE 4.6: Section of pots for collecting date juice

PLATE 4.7: Rice pot

7. Rice pot (*bhater handi*) [6]—carinated body, rounded base, height 20 cm., wheel-made to shoulder. Rice pots vary as:

(a) 15 cm. diameter, rim is flaring, externally thickened, with flat top; constricted neck, sloping shoulder.
(b) 14 cm. diameter, rim is outturned and externally thickened, constricted neck, rounded shoulder.
(c) 15 cm. diameter, outturned and externally thickened rounded rim, constricted neck, sloping shoulder.
(d) 15 cm. diameter, flaring externally sloping, constricted neck, sloping shoulder.

(e) 14 cm. diameter, everted rim, constricted neck, sloping shoulder.

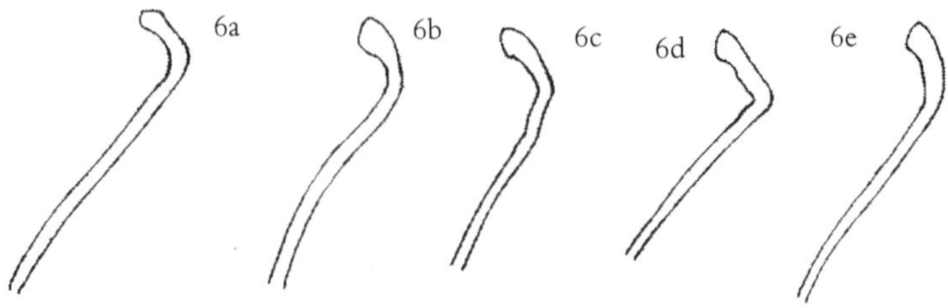

FIGURE 4.7: Section of rice pots

PLATE 4.8: Rice soaking pot

8. Rice soaking pot (*Dhan chhakar handi*) [2]—flaring body, carinated base, 27 cm. height, wheel-made to base and then body widened with paddle and anvil. In this shape examples are:

(a) 16 cm. diameter, flaring and clubbed rim, concave neck, rounded shoulder.
(b) 15 cm. diameter, flaring clubbed rim, concave neck, rounded shoulder.
(c) 16 cm. diameter, outturned, clubbed rim, concave and internally depressed, concave neck, rounded shoulder.
(d) 16.2 cm. diameter, flaring, collared rim, externally ribbed, and internally grooved, concave neck, rounded shoulder.
(e) 15 cm. diameter, flaring clubbed rim, flaring neck, rounded shoulder.

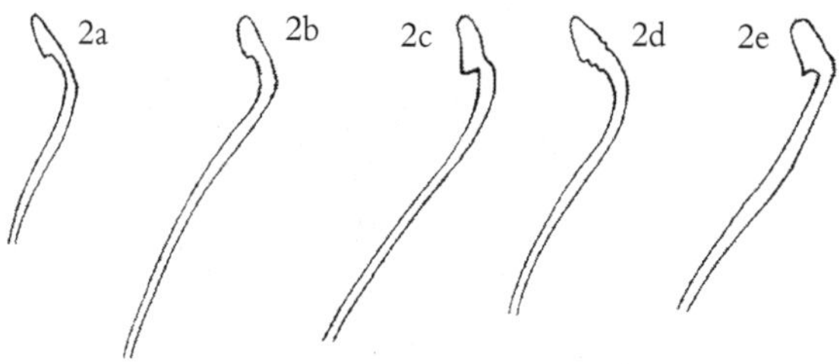

FIGURE 4.8: Section of rice soaking pot

PLATE 4.9: Vegetable pot

9. Vegetable pot (*tarkarir tijel*) used also for boiling milk [9]—partly wheel-made, 15 cm. high, with sharp carination constricted neck, sloping shoulder. Examples are:

    (a) 18 cm. diameter, splayed obliquely, clubbed rounded and internally grooved (two) rim, sharply carinated bicone body.
    (b) 19 cm. diameter, splayed rim, clubbed, straight, and internally grooved; sharply carinated bicone body.
    (c) 17 cm. diameter, splayed rim, clubbed, concave and internally grooved; sharply carinated bicone body.
    (d) 19 cm. diameter, splayed rim, clubbed concave and internally grooved; bulging body.
    (e) 18 cm. diameter, splayed rim, clubbed, concave and internally grooved; bulging body.

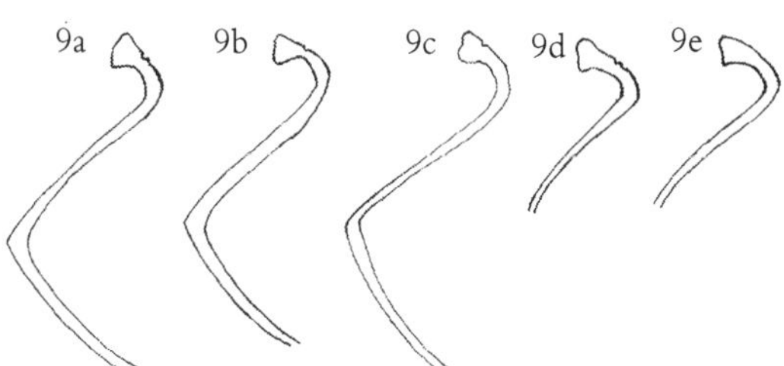

FIGURE 4.9: Section of vegetable pots

PLATE 4.10: *Kunda handi*

10. Ritual pot (*kunda handi* for worshipping Durga with *darpan* or mirror) [10]—completely wheel-made, bulging body tapers down to flat base, 14 cm. height. Rims are incurved, collared and undercut. Bodies are rounded and grooved. Rim variants are:

    (a) 10 cm. diameter rim.
    (b) 10 cm. diameter rim.
    (c) 9 cm. diameter rim.
    (d) 9 cm. diameter rim.
    (e) 10 cm. diameter rim.

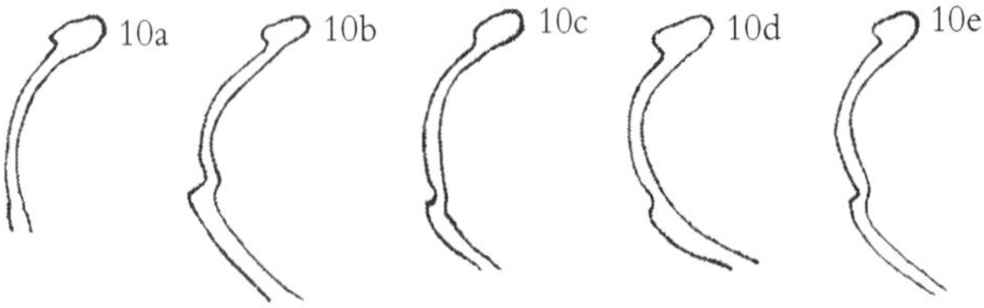

FIGURE 4.10: Section of *kunda handis*

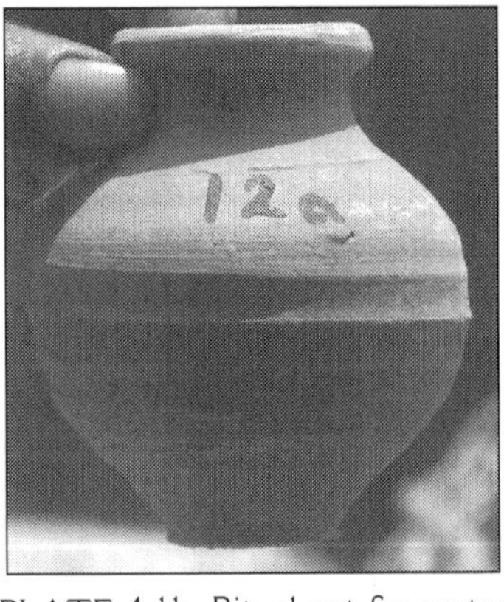

PLATE 4.11: Ritual pot for water

11. Ritual pot (for water) [12]—completely wheel-made. Outturned externally thickened everted rim, concave neck, sloping shoulder and bulging body with corrugation. Variations are as follows.

    (a) 3.6 cm. rim/2.7 cm. base/7.7 cm. height. Plano-convex footed base.
    (b) 3.8 cm. rim/2.3 cm. base/7.2 cm. height. Flat base.
    (c) 3.7 cm. rim/3 cm. base/7.1 cm. height. Flat base.
    (d) 3.7 cm. rim/3 cm. base/7.5 cm. height. Plano-concave base.
    (e) 3.7 cm. rim/2.8 cm. base/7.4 cm. height. Flat footed base.

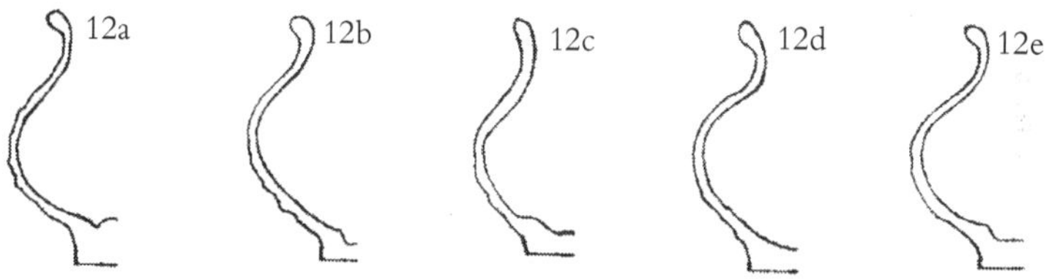

FIGURE 4.11: Section of ritual pots for water

PLATE 4.12: *Kona ghata*

12. Ritual pot (*kona ghata*—for *Ritu* puja) [14]—completely wheel-made. Variants:

    (a) 5.7 cm. rim/1.4 cm. base/5.2 cm. height. Incurved, nailhead and flat rim, bulging body plano-concave base.
    (b) 5.7 cm. rim/3 cm. base/5.3 cm. height. Incurved, externally thickened and flattish rim, bulging body, flat base.
    (c) 5.5 cm. rim/2.9 cm. base/5 cm. height. Incurved, externally thickened and flattish rim, bulging body, flat base.

(d) 5.8 cm. rim/2.8 cm. base/5.1 cm. height. Incurved, externally thickened and flattish rim, bulging body, flat base.
(e) 5.5 cm./3.4 cm. base/5.2 cm. height. Incurved, externally thickened and flattish rim, bulging body, flat base.

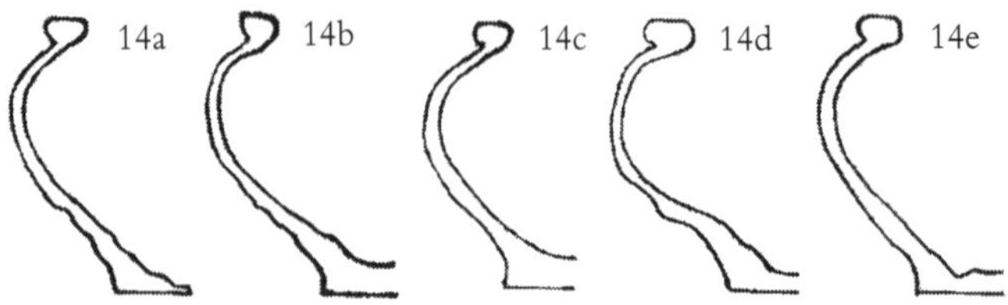

FIGURE 4.12: Section of *kona ghatas*

PLATE 4.13: Offering pot of sweets

13. Ritual pot (*ghata* for offering sweet to the god) [13]—completely wheel-made.

    (a) 6.8 cm. rim/9.7cm. height/4.2 cm. base. Outturned, collared and internally depressed rim, constricted neck, rounded shoulder and body flat internally ribbed base.
    (b) 7 cm. rim/9.6 cm. height/4.4 cm. base. Outturned, collared concave and internally depressed rim, constricted neck, sloping shoulder, rounded body is corrugated near base, flat internally ribbed base.
    (c) 7 cm. rim/9.9 cm. height/4 cm. base. Outturned, clubbed concave and internally depressed rim, constricted neck, rounded shoulder, rounded corrugated body, flat internally ribbed.
    (d) 6.8 cm. rim/10.1 cm. height/4.4 cm. base. Outturned, clubbed concave and internally depressed rim, constricted neck, rounded

shoulder, rounded body is corrugated near base, flat internally ribbed.

(e) 7 cm. rim/9.9 cm. height/3.8 cm. base. Outturned, collared and internally depressed rim, constricted neck, rounded shoulder and body, flat internally ribbed base.

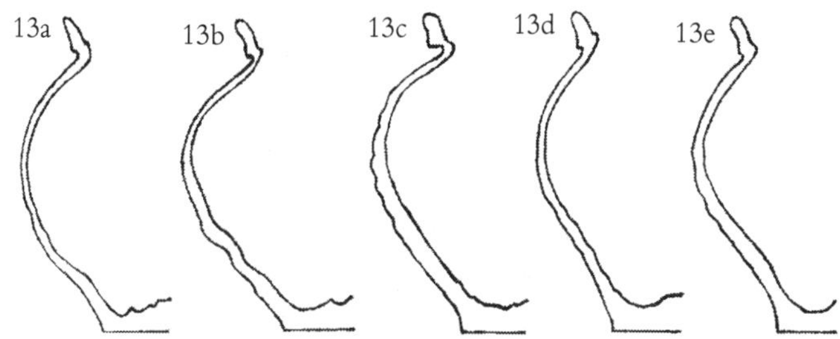

FIGURE 4.13: Section of sweet offering pot

PLATE 4.14: Pot for collecting palmyra palm juice

14. Pot for collecting palmyra palm juice [1]—height 16 cm. Wheel made to shoulder.

 (a) 13.5 cm. diameter, outturned, thick and everted rim, constricted neck, sloping shoulder, rounded body.
 (b) 14 cm. diameter, outturned, thick and everted rim, constricted neck, sloping shoulder, rounded body.
 (c) 13.7 cm. diameter, outturned, thick and everted rim, constricted neck, sloping shoulder, rounded body.
 (d) 13.8 cm. diameter, outturned, thick and everted rim, constricted neck, sloping shoulder, rounded body.
 (e) 13.9 cm. diameter, outturned, thick and everted rim, constricted neck, sloping shoulder, rounded body.

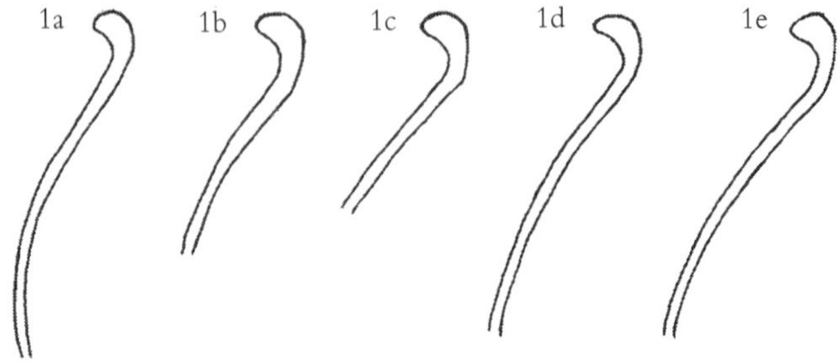

FIGURE 4.14: Section of pots for collecting palmyra palm juice

15. Serving bowl (21)—10 cm. rim/2.8 cm. base/2.9 cm. height, outcurved thickened internally sloping rim, tapering body, flat base.

FIGURE 4.15: Section of serving bowl

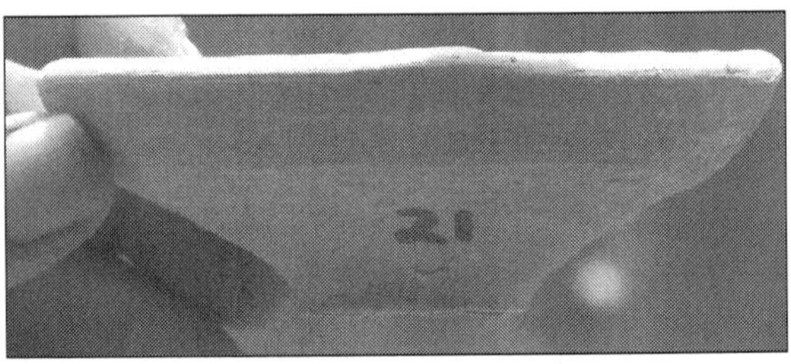

PLATE 4.15: Serving bowl

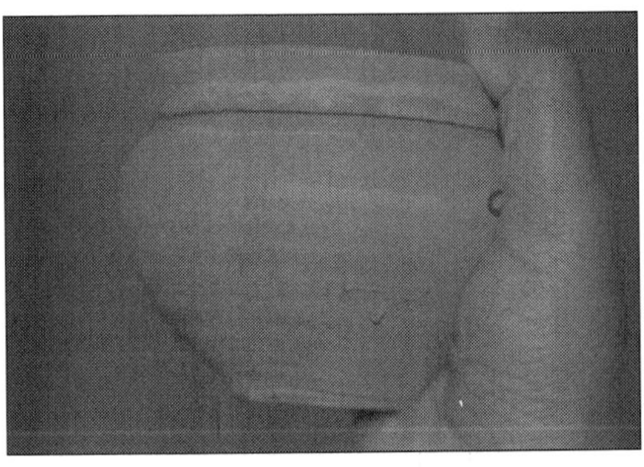

PLATE 4.16: *Rachna handi*

16. Pot for worship as well as cooking rice for a child (*rachna handi*) [11]—

    (a) 10 cm. rim/7.6 cm. height/4.8 cm. base. Flaring and collared rim, constricted neck, rounded shoulder, rounded body, flat base.
    (b) 9.7 cm. rim/7.6 cm. height/4.4 cm. base. Flaring and collared rim, constricted neck, rounded shoulder, tapering body, flat internally knobbed base.
    (c) 9.9 cm. rim/7.4 cm. height/4.5 cm. base. Flaring and collared rim, constricted neck, rounded shoulder, tapering body, flat base.
    (d) 9.4 cm. rim/7.2 cm. height/4.3 cm. base. Flaring and collared rim, constricted neck, rounded shoulder, tapering body, flat base.
    (e) 9.7 cm. rim/7.6 cm. height/4.2 cm. base. Flaring and collared rim, constricted neck, rounded shoulder, rounded body, flat internally knobbed base.

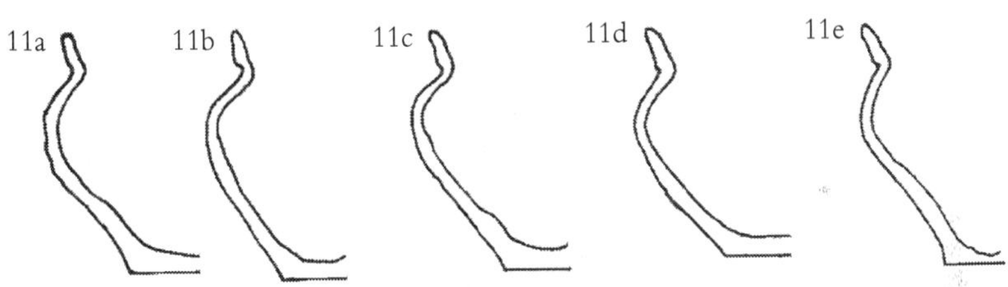

FIGURE 4.16: Section of *rachna handis*

The earlier description was from one shop, its wares manufactured by a single potter. Another shop was chosen to look for differences between two potters catering to same group of consumers. However, all the items were not present and a one-to-one correlation could not be made. Some new types were also noticed which are described but no comparison has been made.

17. Ritual pot (*shanti ghata*) [13]—

    (a) 13 cm. diameter, flaring, externally thickened and triangular rim, tapering neck, rounded shoulder and body.
    (b) 14 cm. diameter, flaring, externally thickened, triangular and slightly drooping rim, tapering neck, sloping shoulder, rounded body.
    (c) 8.6 cm. diameter, collared and externally concave rim, constricted neck, rounded shoulder and body flat base.

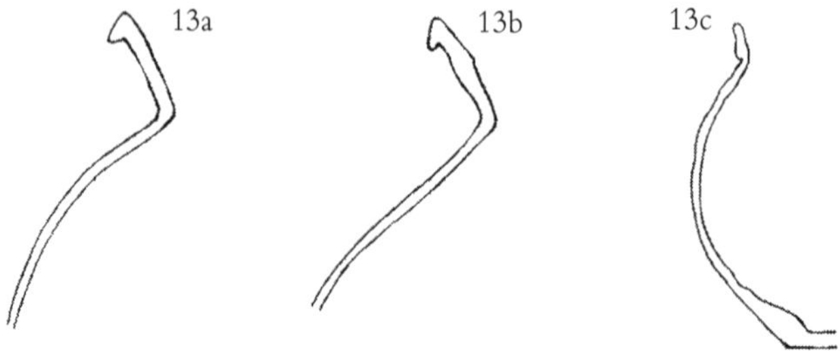

FIGURE 4.17: Sections of *shanti ghatas*

18. Rice pot (*bhater handi*) [6]—

    (a) 19 cm. diameter, flaring and featureless rim, constricted neck, rounded shoulder and body.
    (b) 20 cm. diameter, outturned and clubbed rim, constricted neck, flaring body, round base.
    (c) 19 cm. diameter, outturned and clubbed rim, constricted neck, flaring body, round base.

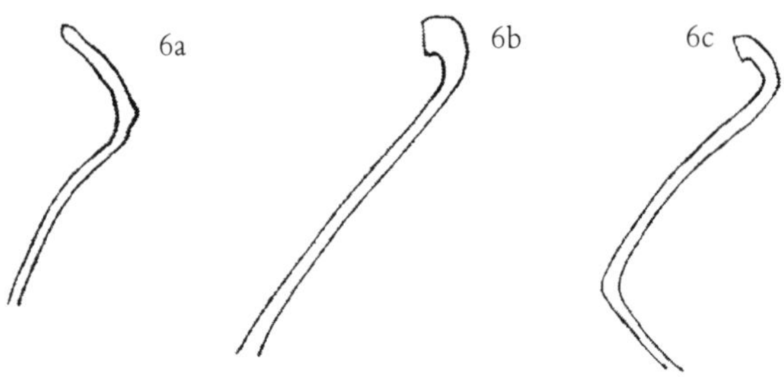

FIGURE 4.18: Sections of rice pot

19. Pot for curd (*daiyer handi*)—19 cm. diameter, outturned clubbed flat rim, tapering neck, concave shoulder, bicone body, rounded base.
20. Pot for collecting palmyra palm juice [22]—13 cm. diameter, splayed obliquely, short and externally thickened rim, constricted neck, sloping shoulder.

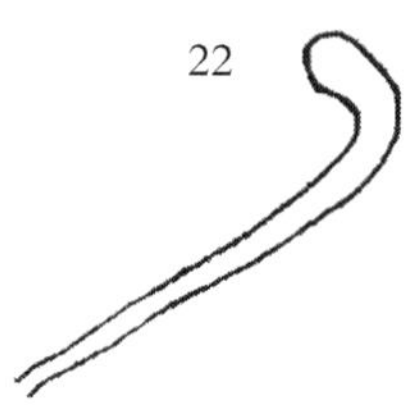

FIGURE 4.19: Section of palmyra palm juice collecting pot

21. Water pitcher (*jaler kalshi*) [4]—

    (a) 14.5 cm. diameter, flaring, externally thick and drooping rim, tapering neck, sloping shoulder.
    (b) 13.5 cm. diameter, flaring, externally thick triangular and drooping rim, tapering neck, sloping shoulder.
    (c) 14 cm. diameter, flaring, clubbed straight rim, concave neck rim, sloping shoulder.

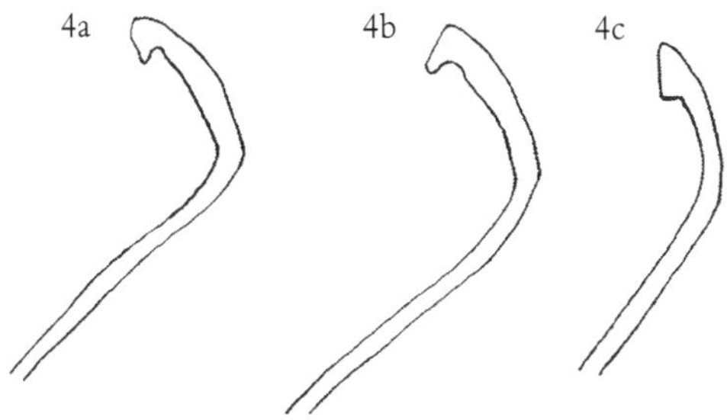

FIGURE 4.20: Section of pitcher of a different potter

22. Pot for storing date juice [23]—13 cm. flaring clubbed rim, concave neck, rounded shoulder, rounded body.

PLATE 4.17: Pot for storing date juice

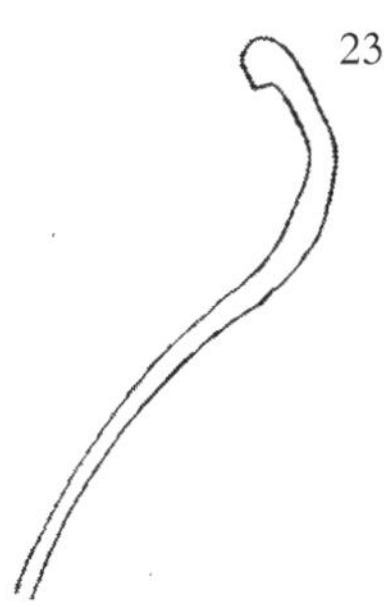

FIGURE 4.21: Section of pot for storing date juice of a different potter

23. Pot for vegetable curry (*tijel*) [9]—

    (a) 18 cm. diameter, flaring and internally sharp rim, constricted neck, slightly carinated shoulder, bicone body and rounded base.
    (b) 18 cm. diameter, flaring and featureless rim, constricted neck, slightly carinated shoulder, bicone body and rounded base
    (c) 22 cm. diameter, flaring, clubbed and internally grooved rim, constricted neck, slightly carinated shoulder, bicone body and rounded base

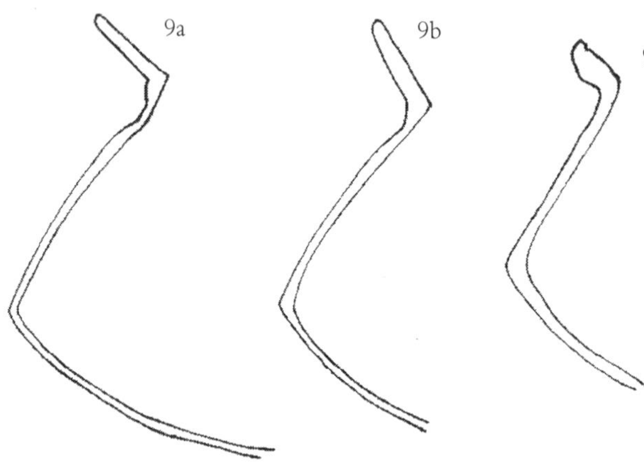

FIGURE 4.22: Section of *tijel*

24. Pot for water (*jaler dabar*) [7]—12 cm. diameter, outturned, clubbed and externally sloping rim with internal depression, concave neck.

FIGURE 4.23: Section of water pot

PLATE 4.18: Water pot

25. Pot for bird's nest (*pakhir basa*) [24]—18.5 cm. diameter, outturned, clubbed rim with grooved top, constricted neck, sloping shoulder, bicone body, rounded base.

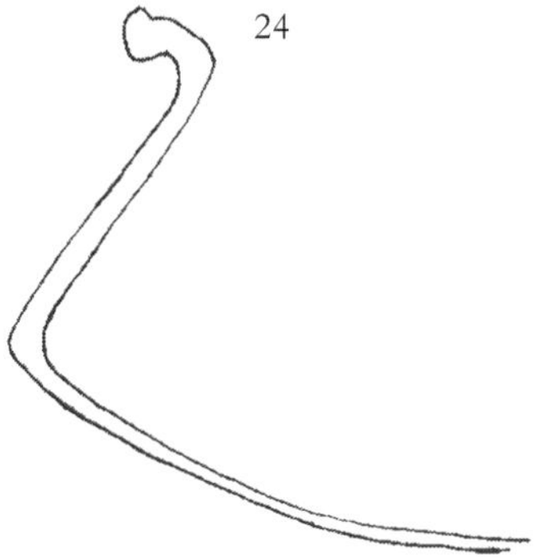

FIGURE 4.24: Section of pot for bird's nest

26. Pot for making pancakes for Muslims (*Musalmander pithe tairir handi*) [25]—22cm. diameter, outcurved and featureless rim, constricted neck, rounded body and base.

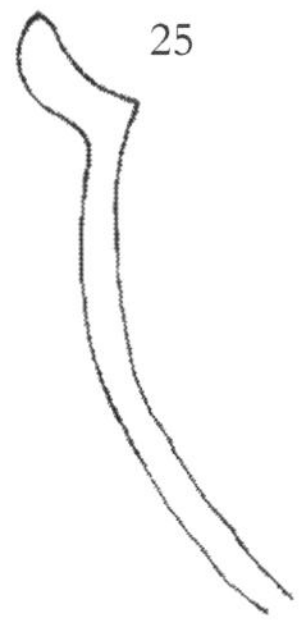

FIGURE 4.25: Section of pot for pancakes

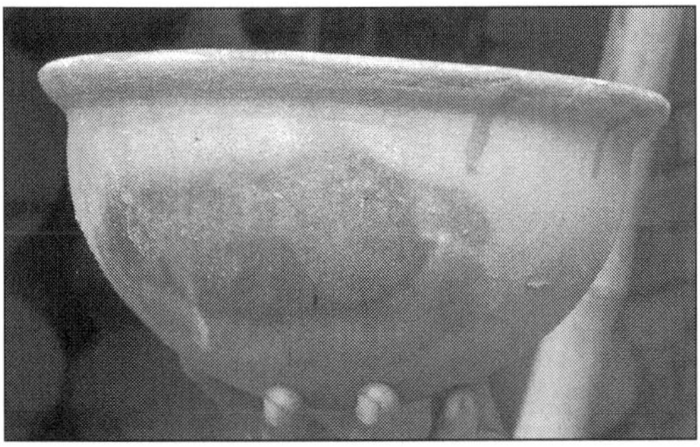

PLATE 4.20: Pot for making pancakes

27. Pot used by Hindus for pancakes (*saru chugli handi*) [26]—22 cm. diameter, obliquely splayed rim, constricted neck, carinated shoulder, flaring body and rounded base.

FIGURE 4.26: Section of pot for pancakes

PLATE 4.21: Pot for pancakes

28. Pot for roasting paddy (*dhan chalar handi*) [2]—

    (a) 17 cm. diameter, outturned, clubbed rim, flattened externally and internally depressed; constricted neck, sloping shoulder.
    (b) 17 cm. diameter, outturned, clubbed rim beveled at the front; constricted neck, sloping shoulder.

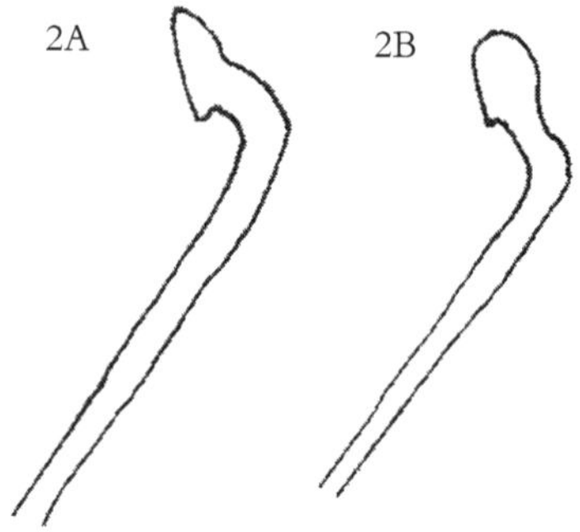

FIGURE 4.27: Section of pot for roasting paddy

VARIATION IN TYPE AND SIZE

From the discussion in this chapter on the variations present in each type, we can see that in some cases there are many while in some others there are very few.

Dishes found in the first shop are very similar in shape though slightly uneven as may be associated with handmade shape. Only one is of distinctively bigger size. The wheel-made water pitcher by contrast is remarkably similar in shape and rim diameter, differing within 1.5 cm. However, there are significant differences between two shops so far as the rim diameter and shape is concerned. There were also small differences between each shape in the second shop.

Another type of pitcher, which is also used for storing date juice, also shows slight distinction and can be perceived as two groups (Fig. 4.3). Both varieties are also noticed in another shop, with minor difference in rim shape.

The water jars (*jaler dabar*) from the first shop are almost the same in size as well as in shape. The other shop has rim shapes distinctly different from the first as also a rim diameter of 12 cm. against 10 cm. There is also a distinct variety that comes from Beral in Medinipur district. This has a black slip with a flaring rim, sharply carinated shoulder and flattish base.

The pots for water (*jaler bhand*) are again very similar but the pots for collecting palm juice (*raser bhand*) show small variations and one is very different from the rest. The shopkeeper claimed that it is made by the same potter. In that case was it made at a different time?

There are also cases where there are very small differences between shapes, with one member slightly different than the rest. Examples of such types are rice pot [No. 7(6)], rice soaking pot [No. 8(2)], vegetable cooking pot [No. 9(9)] and the water pot [No. 3(7)]. It is not always easy to discern if these are general differences for a specific reason. The presence of a groove is certainly deliberate. These otherwise similar shapes look very much to be the work of same potter as claimed by the shopkeeper. Is it potters artistic afterthought to produce a different pot at one time or was it made at a different sitting?

The second shop had of two types of rice pot. One type is similar to the first shop but has a featureless rim instead of externally thickened rim of the first. So is vegetable cooking pot which has one type similar to the first but of slightly larger size and another type with differently shaped rim.

All the ritual pots—*kunda handi, kona ghat, biyer bhand, pujar ghat*—show a remarkable similarity within their respective groups.

There seem to be two size groups present in the market. Two size groups were seen in the rice pot (14–15 cm. and 19–20 cm.), vegetable cooking pots (17–19 cm. and 22 cm.) and water pitchers (12 cm. and 13–15 cm.). These examples are wheel-made. These are also associated with difference in rim shape which could be significant or small. For the pitcher the two groups are not different, so far as the rim shape is concerned, and not associated with increased capacity of the vessel.

In his work on Central Indian pottery, Daniel Miller (1985) tried to look into categorization process of villagers and its connection with the pottery manufactured. His pottery drawings of cooking pots (1985: 42, Fig. 9) suggests a variation in rim types within a category, and it seems that the variability of the rim shapes is reflected in the size of the pot.

However, at Mai-Bibir Hat no such strong affiliation was noticed. Within the same group there is not more than 2 cm. difference in rim diameter irrespective of the size of the vessel. Among pots for collecting palm juice [No. 16(15)] from a single shop produced by a single potter, there are a lot of variations and the rim size ranges from 11.5 to 13 cm. A strong similarity is seen in *kunda handi* [No. 10(10)] with rim sizes ranging between 17 and 19 cm., *kona ghat* [No. 11(12)] with rim sizes 3.6–3.8 cm. and also the pot for storing palm juice [No. 14(1) with rim sizes 9.5–10 cm.

The important finding of this laborious exercise is this. In spite of apparent standardization there is a possibility of coexistence of different shapes within a market which is culturally homogenous. Also the products of one potter might have very small differences that get noticed when drawings are made and could be described as different subtypes in archaeological literature. Such standardization in shape and size might differ from village to village even among full-time potters.

5

Manufacturing Process

MANUFACTURING PROCESS of ceramics has often been described by anthropologists and archaeologists and even by artists working on ceramics. The first elaborate survey on manufacturing process across India was undertaken by Anthropological Survey of India under N.K. Bose who was the then Director; it came out in the form of a book by Saraswati and Behura (1966). The manufacturing process described in archaeological literature is usually area specific and theme oriented. Kramer (1997) tries to illustrate the division of labour and spatial distribution of activity. Miller (1985) discussed manufacturing techniques more generally as the potter's routine. He incidentally found some divergence in manufacturing method in central India from what was described by Saraswati and Behura (1966) and contended that the trends suggested by the latter are not always true. Anup Mishra (2008) similarly tried to understand the pottery technique of Chalcolithic Balathal (Rajasthan) through a detailed ethnographic study of techniques in present-day villages of the region. He (2006) also worked in Malwa (central India) with the view to understand technology of chalcolithic pottery of the area.

The manufacturing process described here, as observed in various parts of West Bengal, aims to trace the process of generation of variability in forms. These formative stages might apparently have little direct bearing on the end product or the range of products. But these variations are fine threads of cultural behaviour which ultimately result in a distinct creation. The context of such activity though important is little understood. Not all aspects of such behaviour are revealed by this survey because it is not intensive enough to understand processes at the level of individuals and households. A survey, such as this, covering very small regions of four districts of West Bengal would not be able to reveal all the threads of the matrix. However, it might give some insights into the process.

Different methods were encountered for the preparation of the clay. Usually clay from the field forms the basic ingredient. In South 24 Parganas district, where local clay is very fine, for making the base of a rice cooking pot or a vegetable cooking pot, reddish course grained sand (*lal bali*) is brought from Arambagh (Hugli district, on the right bank of Hugli River),

126 km. as the crow flies. In Malda, soil is usually obtained from local fields or brought by truck from outside the village; but within the district, in which case there is no fixed place and potters are not sure about the region, sand is obtained from the river. In Nastika, Birbhum, clay from the Manikarnika riverbed which is not fine, is again mixed with coarse sand acquired from the Mayurakshi River. At Batashpur the clay is procured from a local pond and only sand is procured from Manikarnika. At Mahula both soil and sand are collected from the Kopai River. At Bishaypur the clay was collected from local pond, the sand is from the Mayurakshi. In Bardhaman most of the clay is acquired from the local pond and lakes. Therefore, it is clear that the people of each area try to make the best out of local resources. However, when it is not sufficient or some ingredient is not available locally, they may acquire it from elsewhere and may even be willing to bring it from afar.

In most places the clay collected would be further treated. Usually the large impurities are picked out. The clay is kneaded and adequate water is added to the dough before it is wedged and thrown on the wheel. Only in a single village in North 24 Parganas (Bamanmura) was levigation in evidence: the clay is thrown in a square tank of water and the heavier particles sink and settle first. In most cases the women of the house prepare the clay. Kneading may be done by hand, and sometimes even the feet, at a primary stage. In some villages the kneaded clay was again cut into small parts with a string and re-kneaded for uniformity of texture, e.g. at Gorerhat, South 24 Parganas. The same technique was also noticed at Bonpara, Bardhaman.

The addition of tempering material to the clay paste is dependent on the function the vessel is expected to perform. In South 24 Parganas the clay used for the base of the *handis* and pans is tempered with large-grained sand to withstand the heat of every day cooking. Paddy husk is used as temper for basins. In Malda the entire vessel has more sand and paste for making the *tawa* that is used by the Muslims to make *roti* are even grittier. For smaller clay items like money pots, the lump of clay is tempered with sand and ash. Water vessels are treated only with sand. Sometimes sand is applied on the outside and not mixed into the clay. In Birbhum, all the vessels, pitchers or pans, are made of the same kind of paste. This is a mixture of the slightly coarse grained clay with sand.

The slip is an integral part of the pottery making process. Usually it is prepared separately by individual households for their own use. The ingredient, however, is acquired locally or otherwise. In some cases it is bought in a market. In that case the initial stages of preparation are already done. The prepared matter for the slip is usually dried before being sold. At Raghunathbari, East Medinipur district, inhabited by a large potter community, the slip is prepared at an industrial scale (Pl. 5.1). But the market for this is not restricted to the village and goes far into South 24 Parganas.

Most of the time the slip consists of the body clay, the same as that used for the pot. A lot more water is added to make it slurry. But in South 24 Parganas the slip is also made out of ochrous soil from Medinipur for a better shade of red. Sometime insect nests found near the river are used for a maroonish tint. In Malda district soil comes from neighbouring upland of Bihar or even from a local soil from iron rich old alluvium (Barind). In Bardhaman the soil for the slip comes from the western uplands. Sources of Birbhum are common with that of Bardhaman in many cases.

Various manufacturing methods are used in rural Bengal, shaping by hand or in a mould and wheel throwing. In most cases these are not exclusive of each other. Handmade vessels for the most part are made over other open mouthed vessels and turned around to maintain a round rim and the body is expanded with a dabber (Pl. 5.2). Sometimes the rim is shaped by turning it over another finished pot. These are usually methods for small and medium sized vessels, trays and bowls. But even larger vessels like pitchers and *handis* are manufactured by hand, in which case only the rim is prepared, leaving a lot of clay at the bottom to be beaten with paddle and anvil to the desired shape.

PLATE 5.1: Raghunathbari slip kept in clean pots and covered by broken pots

PLATE 5.2: Handmade pottery with pottery turntable and dabber

Slab work was observed at Ramkrishnapur in Birbhum district, where large jars are produced (Pl. 5.3). A similar method is also used in Bardhaman for large basins. In both cases the base is luted to the body later.

Large jars in South 24 Parganas were produced in a slightly different way. The rim is made on wheel. The shoulder and base and middle part are shaped on a mould seperately. Then the edges of the separate pieces are beaten so that they adhere.

Most of the medium and large sized vessels, that are open-mouthed and round bottomed, are made over a mould. These moulds are found in two types—convex and concave. The concave type is a technological extension of the method that used other open-mouthed vessels as a base (Pl. 5.4). However, these moulds are made on the floor of the workshop. They provide a larger and deeper surface for the large vessels, such as deep pans for frying and dry roasting.

For still larger types like those for feeding cows or soaking rice, convex moulds are used. These are also built on the floor of the workshop (Pl. 5.5). Concave mould was not noticed in South 24 Parganas. While in Malda pottery dice (mould) is more common though not an exclusive method of this region.

The use of wheels was found in all places that were visited. In the west and south there are spoked wheels. At Nakali (South 24 Parganas), two kinds of wheel were observed—one with spokes for making large vessels and a solid disc of cement for making smaller vessels. Usually one vessel is thrown at a time unless they are very small pots, like tea cups. Yet I have found a spoked wheel with a large lump of clay centred on it, from which the upper parts of thirty five *handis* could be made (as claimed by a potter at Tantirhat, Pl. 5.6). In most cases, pitchers and cooking pots are only partly shaped on the wheel.

PLATE 5.3: Ramkrishnapur handmade jar

PLATE 5.4: A vessel is being prepared on a concave mould with a dabber

PLATE 5.5: Convex fixed mould at Thupsara workshop

Solid wheels in use in Malda (Pl. 5.7), make multiple pots from a single centring. The spoked wheel with some innovations has been introduced recently by the government which, the potter proudly claimed, can bear a weight up to 20 kg. of clay.

The lower part of the larger vessels is made separately and attached to the wheel-made upper part. For South 24 Parganas, large grained sand is kneaded with the clay and transformed into round sheets much like an unbaked roti (Pl. 5.8). These are then attached to the upper body by pressing the edges with finger tips. A similar method is also followed in Birbhum and Bardhaman. The upper part is of finer clay and wheel-turned. The lower body is then enlarged with paddle and anvil using river sand which makes the inner side micaceous. However, in Malda the entire vessel is turned on wheel. The body is then enlarged and shaped by beating with a paddle on an anvil. In Birbhum ash is used in place of fine grained sand. This was also noticed at Malda.

Several types of paddle were observed (Pl. 5.9). A paddle with deep grooves is used to attach two pieces, while the plain paddle is used to smooth out the outer side. A chequered paddle with a slightly rounded surface (like jack fruit according to the potter) was also used to strengthen the clay. Similarly different kinds of dabbers are used for shaping and smoothing vessels (Pl. 5.10).

PLATE 5.6: Potter making pots on wheel at Tantirhat

PLATE 5.7: Solid wheel at Krishnapalli

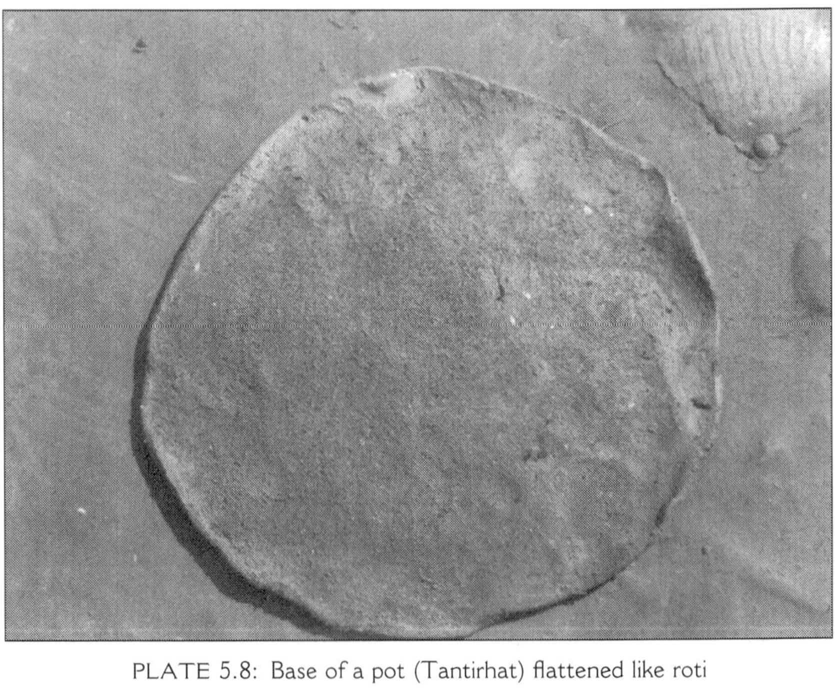

PLATE 5.8: Base of a pot (Tantirhat) flattened like roti

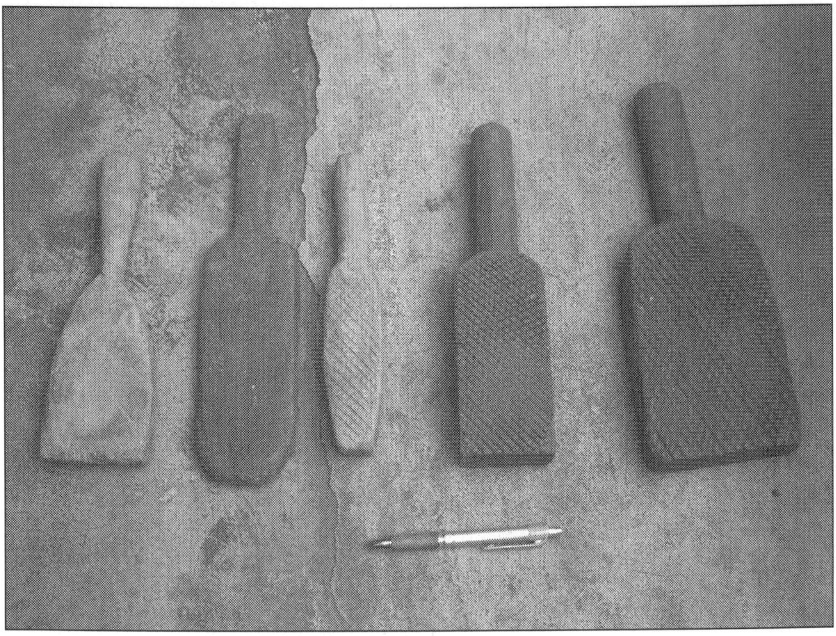

PLATE 5.9: A set of paddles

Drying the vessels before firing is a complex task and usually takes place in the courtyard of the potter's house (Pl. 5.11). In Birbhum, at first the pot is dried under a plastic sheet as a quick loss of water may cause cracks in the vessel. The wheel-made part of a pot or pitcher is partly dried before the lower half is attached. At Bardhaman for the large vessels that are made in parts, the top part is dried first with the rim up. The side that faces up dries faster. After the bottom is attached, it is dried upside down. Similarly, the body of the basin which is made on a convex mould is allowed to dry on it. It is then taken out and the rim is attached. This method is commonly used all over. The moulded pots are usually made

PLATE 5.10: A set of dabbers

PLATE 5.11: Courtyard of a potter's house where pottery is drying

to dry on a stand. This could be another already dried pot or broken top half. In Malda it was observed that handmade pots are partly dried before the lower part is beaten to shape with paddle and anvil. Occasionally a stand made of straw (*bide*) is also used for drying large jars and basins, as at Nakali in South 24 Parganas.

The slip is applied to semi-dried pots with a cloth (Pl. 5.12). It is usually applied on the top half of a pot. At Birbhum the slip is also applied on the interior of the pans for a smoother roasting/frying surface. It is also applied on inner side of dish noticed in South 24 Parganas. At Mathurapur in Malda, an off-white coating of kaolinite clay is applied, above which the slip is applied. Black slips are rare, found in South 24 Parganas on cannabis smoking pipes. This is done by placing the pipes in a pot and stuffing it with acacia leaves, then covering it and placing it inside kiln. Therefore, the firing takes place under a reducing atmosphere. The acacia leaves, it is claimed, bring out a glaze in the pipes. Another method was observed in Bharatpur, Bardhaman district. Here a fired red pot is coated with charcoal and fired again. This also produces a shinning black slip but the core is red. *Murum* or ground laterite is used in Birbhum and Bardhaman and red earth of old alluvium (Barind) in Malda, along with laterite from Rajmahal in Bihar. The maroonish slip of South 24 Parganas comes from insect nests.

Painting is rarely done. Black paint is applied on red slip of pitchers and basins. This colour traditionally comes from a dark clay nodule but more often comes from car battery. These are simple broad horizontal black bands painted on the shoulder. However, ritual pots commonly have painting in dark red or white. In South 24 Parganas only one type of ritual pot (*debi-ghata*) is painted. It is often decorated with many colours including those chemically manufactured.

Incised and stamped decorations are also made. In Malda, pans used by the Muslims for making roti have incised decorations, as also ritual pots of Birbhum. Pitchers from South 24 Parganas have stamped decorations.

Ceramics from all these regions are kiln-fired. I found that the firing process is similar in the villages of south and west. These villages have well constructed kilns, albeit with different structures. Usually, the walls are of mud, occasionally they are also reinforced with brick. These are provided with a channel, the end opening outside being fed with fuel from time to time. This is usually dry wood, straw, or charcoal. But in the western region there is a preference for leaves of palmyra palm.

The method of conducting heat is different in different regions. In the South 24 Parganas, the base on which the pottery is kept is solid. There is a hole on one side linking the pottery to the fore chamber where the fire is lit from where the heat that is generated spreads. In Birbhum and

PLATE 5.12: Application of slip on unbaked pots at Tantirhat

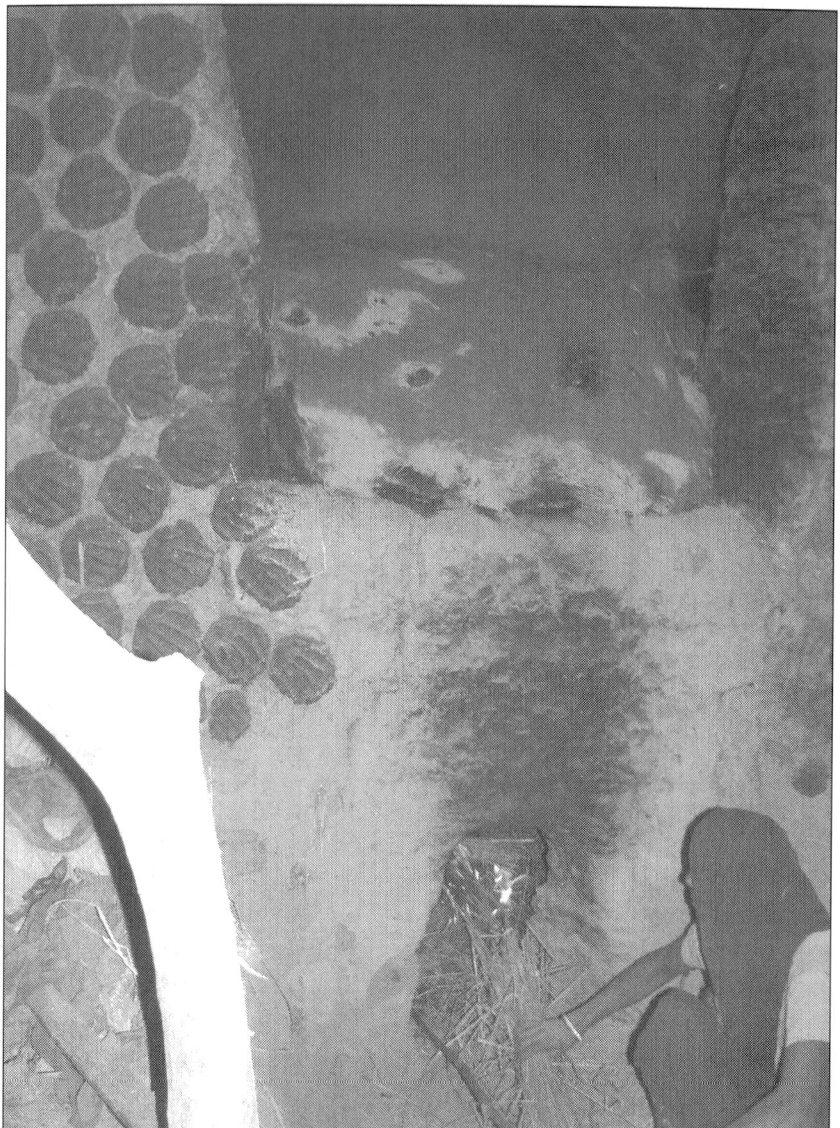

PLATE 5.13: Potter's wife putting straw in kiln

Bardhaman, the pottery is heaped on a stand. This stand has a radial design, round holes arranged in a ring. In Raghunathbati, Medinipur, a kiln was observed, which was dug under the ground with a palm-thatched roof on top. After the pots are arranged in a pile, it is covered with straw and mud. A few holes are left to allow oxygen in. At Malda there are built kilns paved with mud and occasionally brick that have a tiled roof.

However, there is no other permanent feature of the kiln like a channel for fuel or an earthen grill.

It can be surmised from the earlier discussion that a lot of variation in production process is actually due to local conditions. For example, use of coarse sand in the lower part of the vessel is a functional necessity. But at Birbhum the entire pot is made of the same clay because it contains enough sand to survive repeated heating. However, the use of concave and convex moulds is an innovation not linked to physical environment. It is a ready to use device, providing a potter with a smooth hard steady surface for shaping large pots. Most often there are technical choices and why one is preferred over the other cannot be easily explained.

Wheel Throwing

Much of the pottery produced since the chalcolithic period was shaped on the wheel. This section will try to trace the variations that are generated when this is done, and what decisions are made by the potter to bring about these variations.

There are several descriptions of the process of manufacturing pottery on the wheel round the world. Use of wheel to manufacture pots has been considered by Roux and Corbetta (1989) as a mark of specialization. For my part I describe the process to evaluate variations keeping in mind commonly available shapes that are found in archaeological sites. This was documented from a potter at Kashinagar village of South 24 Parganas district.

Ghata

1. A lump of clay is thrown on the centre of the wheel while setting it in motion. The clay is patted down cleared from sides and enlarged on the top; it is smoothed from the sides as it rises up with the rotation of wheel.
2. The left thumb is placed on the top, the palm on the side, and then the thumb pushes down to make a hollow (Pl. 5.14) which is increased in size by inserting the other thumb in. The same action also adds water to the inner side of the pot and the thumbs start exerting pressure on the sides.
3. The rest of the fingertips press at the bottom to increase the height of the clay keeping the side stable.
4. The fingers slide up the sides as the height increases, the thumbs which are inside press outward increasing the girth, which makes the rim incurved and featureless (Pl. 5.15).

PLATE 5.14: Potter making hole on clay

5. The left hand moves to the top, the thumb and first finger is out and the others are inside, supporting the wall. The right hand supports the pot from the exterior. The thumb exerts pressure below the rim. This thickens the rim (Pl. 5.16).
6. The right hand against the exterior applies pressure on the upper part below the rim which causes the mouth to open up and the upper part to constrict to a neck and the lower part to bulge (Pl. 5.17).

PLATE 5.15: Incurved featureless rim

PLATE 5.16: Thickened/collared rim

7. The left fingers move in and the right hand disengages from the top, sliding up the body which causes the piece to gain height.
8. Then thc right hand applies pressure on the bottom which too increases the height by displacing clay from there (Pl. 5.18).
9. The bulge also moves up and forms a sharp carination (Pl. 5.19) as the left thumb rests on the rim and the other fingers on the inside press out the shoulder while the right hand at the bottom on the exterior slides up.

PLATE 5.17: Internal pressure causing the side of the pot to bulge

PLATE 5.18: The hand slide up to increase the height of the pot

10. As the right hand slides up the pot, the carination flattens and gets rounded. The neck portion increases in height.
11. As the right hand is placed on the neck and the fingers of the left hand, press on the inside, the rim flares out (Pl. 20). The left thumb placed on the top of the rim gives it sharpened edge.
12. The hands slide up the rim making it thinner.
13. Pressure is applied from inside by the left hand which cause the body to bulge and right hand applies pressure on the neck defining it further (Pl. 21).

PLATE 5.19: Carination being produced in a pot

PLATE 5.20: Flaring out of rim as pressure is exerted on interior

14. Both the hands are placed on the top with the thumbs on the exterior under the rim and the other fingers in the inside press down to splay out the rim (Pl. 5.22).
15. Then with a short board, slightly curved, of areca-nut stem in the right hand, pressure is applied on the exterior and in the interior on the shoulder with left hand, so that the clay is drawn upwards

PLATE 5.21: The neck of the pot being defined

PLATE 5.22: The rim is splayed out

by the left hand giving the body a *ghata* shape with short concave neck, bulging body, and short splayed rim.

16. The clay is again brought up from inside and the board is pressed against the underside of the rim as the clay slopes down. Then it is pressed back on rim at an angle making it triangular and clubbed in shape (Pl. 5.23).
17. When the angle is straightened the rim becomes clubbed and square. Drawing out more clay from interior, the exterior gets rounded up to collared (Pl. 5.24).

PLATE 5.23: Clubbed triangular rim

PLATE 5.24: Collared rim

Vase

The first two steps are the same as per the *ghata*.

3. Some small changes to previous hand movements were made by sliding the hands up the mouth and retaining the opening that was created. The rim shape, still slightly incurved and internally sloping is further straightened. The next actions are also similar, the right hand applying more pressure and increasing the height in a swift single motion.

The next action is similar to stages 4, 5, 6 and 7 (Pl. 5.25) mentioned earlier.

8. Then the stem is pressed at the base with right hand and the left hand slowly moves up interior. This makes the pot round up in the middle (Pl. 5.26). The stem gives a smoother surface than fingers. While it shapes the lower part to shoulder, the left hand supports the neck.
9. Then it moves down to apply pressure on the middle, enlarging the body.
10. The stem is then brought up to the neck which turns the later to constricted form.
11. The stem is pressed under and fingers pressing out from inside the rim, giving it a flare.
12. The left hand with the thumb and the first finger out and other fingers placed above the rim, slope the clay from inside down the edge of the rim making a collar.

PLATE 5.25: From a rounded body the pot is getting elongated (vase)

13. Then the left thumb is placed under the rim exerting pressure and the fingers inside. The clay is shifted up making the rim clubbed. The first finger of the right hand presses the rim on the exterior flattening the front.
14. But making a groove on the exterior of the rim with a sharp tool failed.
15. Then the left hand was placed on top of the rim to exert pressure and the stem below for support and make a horizontally splayed rim but it sliced the neck slightly.

PLATE 5.26: Pressure is being exerted on the base of the neck to bulge up the body

PLATE 5.27: Neck is constricted

16. In the next attempt the mouth was kept closed then. After addition of some more water, placing the right thumb on the exterior and the first and the second finger on the interior, rim was bent slowly from outturned, to flaring, obliquely splayed, and horizontally splayed in turn.
17. Then fingers placed inside slide out and down to make the rim droop.
18. Thereafter, the drooping rim was folded, giving it a rounded shape and groove (Pl. 5.28). It was not a uniform groove.

Bowl

1. A lump of clay is thrown on the centre of the wheel while setting it in motion. The clay is potted down cleared from sides and enlarged on the top; it is smoothed from the sides as it rises up with the rotation of wheel.
2. After centring as the height piled up (Pl. 5.29), the left thumb plunged down the clay. The right thumb also moves in.
3. The opening is increased size but not to the extent as seen previously in the case of *ghata* and the vase.
4. As the fingers on the exterior touch the base it does not allow the clay to spread making the wall thick (Pl. 5.30).
5. Then the thumbs press outward, enlarging the body.
6. The thumbs from inside and the fingers from the exterior, slide upward and slightly outward enlarging the mouth and the body.
7. With the areca-nut stem, slight pressure is applied on top of the rim due to which it first becomes everted (Pl. 5.31), then

PLATE 5.28: Making groove on the rim

outturned as the left hand slides up some clay from inside, and then internally sloping the right forefinger on lip ultimately makes it flat topped.

Vase 2

1. The clay is centred and patted flat to spread out over a larger area than in the case of vase 1.
2. Then as the wheel rotates both the hands are placed on top and the clay spreads in a way that the heap rise from the bed at a low angle.

PLATE 5.29: The clay is about to be pierced

PLATE 5.30: The clay is concentrated on the wall

3. The left thumb is pushed down the clay followed by the right thumb (in a single movement, adding water to the interior of the clay).
4. Again by exerting pressure outward by thumbs and downwards by the fingers placed in the exterior, a wide mouthed cylinder is formed (Pl. 5.32).
5. Then the left forefinger and thumb are placed across the rim and the right hand presses the wall just below the rim to accumulate the clay from neck onwards and to close the mouth (Pl. 5.33). The pressure from the thumb below the rim thickens it externally.

PLATE 5.31: The everted rim

PLATE 5.32: Wide mouthed cylindrical clay

6. Then the fingers of the left hand are placed in to support the interior and the right hand supports the exterior from the base. The clay structure is elongated as the fingers move up.
7. The left hand is again placed across the mouth. The neck is straightened and the rim is thickened (Pl. 5.34).
8. The areca stalk is introduced and slowly brought up to the rim, with pressure (Pl. 5.35), the left hand in the interior also moves

PLATE 5.33: Thickening of rim

PLATE 5.34: The elongation of clay structures and thickening of rim

up to the neck putting pressure in turn which again makes the rim funnel shaped (Pl. 5.36).

9. Then the forefinger of the right hand is placed on top of the rim with the left thumb under the rim and the fingers inside bend it down. The rim gets splayed and then droops down.
10. Again thumb and the forefingers of the left hand are placed across the rim making it collared and rounded.

PLATE 5.35: The neck is elongated as the left hand slides up and right hand supports shoulder

PLATE 5.36: Funnel shaped neck

11. The areca stem is placed on the base vertically with right hand and the left hand goes in applying pressure outward. This make the contour of the body rounded.
12. Then again the stem is placed horizontally at the base of the rim to support it. The left thumb and forefinger are placed across it, apply pressure as it flares out and then bends down to form horizontally a splayed rim, concave neck, and rounded shoulder (Pl. 5.37).

PLATE 5.37: Horizontally splayed rim

PLATE 5.38: The centred and tapped down clay

Vase 3

1. The clay is centred and spread over a large area as in the above case (Pl. 5.38).
2. The mouth of the vessel is opened with the left thumb pushed in followed by the right thumb after adding some water to the clay.
3. Then the clay is made to rise off the base and the mouth is widened.
4. As the clay is made to rise further, the mouth gets constricted (Pl. 5.39) and clay is made to accumulate at the rim with the

PLATE 5.39: Pressure applied to constrict the neck and open up the rim

PLATE 5.40: Pressure is applied to flare out the rim

right hand pressing the rising clay down and the left forefinger and thumb supporting the underside of the rim.

5. Then the right hand is placed under the rim and the left on top and interior, applying pressure which flares and thins out the rim and constricts the neck further (Pl. 5.40).
6. Then the left hand presses the rim down as the right supports the wall under the rim, and splaying it out (Pl. 5.41).

PLATE 5.41: Splayed rim

PLATE 5.42: Pressed down to form drooping rim

7. The left hand goes in and pushes the body outward as the right hand holds the areca stalk and supports the outer body of the pot, thus enlarging the body while keeping the neck narrow.
8. The splayed rim is then pushed down making the drooping rim (Pl. 5.42).
9. While the left hand pressed the rim further out and down the right hand holding the stem provided support giving it the final form (Pl. 5.43).

PLATE 5.43: The areca stem is placed under the rim for support while giving a final shape

PLATE 5.44: Opening up the mouth with inserted fingers

Basin/bowl

1. The centred clay is formed into a rounded cone.
2. The centred clay is opened up with thumb but the fingers do not allow the clay to spread or to rise making the wall thick (Pl. 5.44).
3. Then pressure is applied outward, enlarging the body, making it convex.
4. The left thumb and forefinger is placed on the exterior and the rim is lodged between the first and second finger as the fingers inside continue to displace clay from inside to exterior enlarging the cavity. This makes the body convex and the clay accumulate on the inner side so that the rim is internally thickened (Pl. 5.45).

PLATE 5.45: Convex body internally thickened rim

PLATE 5.46: The rim is thickened

5. The body is straightened up as clay from inner and outer sides gather externally on the rim and is lodged between fingers of the left hand, those placed inside giving support and right hand fingers drawing clay from base upwards (Pl. 5.46).
6. The thumb of the left hand is placed externally under the rim and other fingers push the inner wall. The right hand placed on the lower part causes the clay to rise and form a carination on the body.
7. As the right hand slides up, the body of the bowl takes a rounded form (Pl. 5.47).

PLATE 5.47: Right hand rounding up the body and left hand supporting from inside

PLATE 5.48: The rim is outturned

8. Then the first finger of the right hand presses down the rim, the left thumb remains under the rim. The rim bends and folds down (Pl. 5.48).
9. The size of the pot is increased by exerting pressure outward.
10. The left thumb supports the rim from below, while the forefinger draws the clay outward. The right hand presses the rim down. This caused the mouth to ultimately fold up to into a collared rim (Pl. 5.49).

PLATE 5.49: The rim is pressed down to become collared

PLATE 5.50: The hole is pierced on the centred clay

Handi

1. The centred clay is patted flat and made to spread.
2. Then the hole is made for the mouth (Pl. 5.50).
3. The height increases and hands slide up closing the mouth as outward pressure is maintained by the fingers inside.
4. Then the left hand gently opens up the rim and the right hand on the sides which straightens the rim and the body.
5. The left thumb and the first finger are placed across the rim with thumb at the base of the rim, thickening it.
6. The body again increases in size as the right hand presses the pot near the neck and the left hand pushes outwards. As the body bulges, the mouth gets constricted (Pl. 5.51).

PLATE 5.51: The mouth is constricted and a carination is formed

7. Then the stem slides up the body and the left hand pulls out the clay and the rim. The stem is placed vertically, it smoothens the sloping shoulder and maintains the carination. The left hand continues to bend down the rim as the thumb supports the neck and the right forefinger joins in to splay out the rim (Pl. 5.52).

Dish

With similar steps (stages 1–3) the centred clay is transformed into thickish bowl with incurved rim.

4. Left fingers slide across the bowl as the height increases, and opens up the mouth.
5. The fingers are placed under the rim to increase its thickness.
6. The right and left hands slide up the body, flaring out the rim (Pl. 5.53).
7. The tip of the rim is flattened with finger of left hand.
8. Then right palm is placed flat on the exterior and the left on the interior wall applies pressure to flatten the sides and further open up the mouth (Pl. 5.54).
9. The stem is placed on the centre and drawn outward to of latten the sides almost to the level of the base (Pl. 5.55).
10. An attempt was made to raise the corner and transform that into side of the dish (the rim is much lower than the handmade variety) (Pl. 5.56).

PLATE 5.52: Obliquely splayed rim

PLATE 5.53: The body is flared out while clay is accumulated on the rim

Initiating Changes

It seems from the earlier discussion on manufacturing that the first adjustments are made according to the vessel size and base size. The base or girth size (in case of pots partly made on wheel) would guide the spread of the centred clay. The desired size of the body (diameter) would guide how much openness would be maintained before the height of the vessel

PLATE 5.54: The sides are pressed down

PLATE 5.55: Clay is gathered from inner side to the edge

is increased. The enlargement of the vessel girth precedes the constriction of the neck in the case of larger forms.

For making a bowl, with a small base and a small body, the clay is piled high. The hole is increased but not as much as for vases. Usually, a large number of tea cups are produced from a single centring. In this case, since a single bowl would be made, the fingers placed on the exterior do not allow the clay to spread out or rise. In case of the basin, the lump of clay is broad based. The treatment of the body is similar.

PLATE 5.56: Completed dish

The simplest rim form is the incurved featureless rim, which is made by a single movement of enlarging the mouth and the body. Internal thickening happens in the rim as the clay drawn up the finger from the inner side gets accumulated slightly below the top of the rim. The rim is everted in the process of smoothing the rim top.

The thicker kind of rim needs early decision especially in case of vessels with lower height. In case of taller vessels the height is usually achieved first and as the body is shaped, the rim accumulates clay. But the shape of the rim will decide how much should be accumulated. The successful execution of unknown shapes may nevertheless still be difficult.

The accumulated clay at the top would produce a thickened or externally thickened rim in an action that delineates the rim from rest of the body before the shaping of the body is completed. Before the pot is finished, the rim shape is usually finalized. The clay drawn from inside is sloped out, making an externally thickened sloping rim. To make a short splayed rim a stem of areca nut or finger is placed on top which bends the rim. A thickened rim may be guided by the areca nut stem to a more definitive shape with triangular or straight sided projection—clubbed triangular or clubbed square forms. When some more clay is drawn up the interior the exterior is rounded up and the rim is collared. By supporting the base of the rim and pushing down the interior the rim is horizontally splayed. This can be pushed further down to form drooping rim. It seems that collared forms and clubbed forms can be shaped later from a drooping form but probably would be done earlier if those are the shape the potter is aiming to produce.

Problems Faced

It was noticed that while the artisan was manufacturing these shapes, he faced some problems.

1. It is not easy to place the groove in the correct place.
2. Make an externally drooping rim, or even.
3. Basic forms like the tapering body and dish with incurved rim.

Roux and Corbetta (1989) have characterized the complexity of wheel throwing into mastery of physical parameters, mastery over motor parameters and understanding of relationships which determine succession of different fashioning operations. The first two factors lie with the potter who is at the wheel regularly and successfully. But if shapes given are somewhat new, he makes mistakes. Some he could rectify in the second attempt but most, he could not. These would require a few more trials to eliminate errors. This is not a reflection of his skill but the extent to which his motor functions are not guided by conscious decisions. This is in a sense a degree of specialization which almost amounts to mechanical actions.

In the context of household craft production, the process of creation of this mental template starts from the visual pattern generated in childhood and develops through apprenticeship as he physically develops. The process is only further strengthened as the same vessel forms are produced day in and day out. Potters from all the regions under survey prefer to make one type of pot at a time and even one size at a time. Therefore, changes will be introduced only if there is a strong incentive. Therefore, significant variation in pottery assemblage would suggest a change in the socio-cultural system which could induce it, i.e. as an introduction of new food, which may require a different type of vessel for processing. It could be a change in taste, of shape, or decoration, which may be due to either internal or external causes.

6

Conclusion

FORM AND VARIATION

THIS STUDY HAS ATTEMPTED to explore variations generated in the production of present-day pottery. These variations include differences in morphometry and form in different regions, within a locality and in the same workshop. The manufacturing methods that produced these pottery types were also studied. A specific study was made of shaping on the wheel to see what kinds of moves of the hand give rise to different shapes.

The present survey shows that at a primary level the variations are determined by function. The basic morphometry is guided by the function a pot is expected to perform. Basins and *muri* roasters are both open mouthed vessels. But rim to height ratio for the basin is about 5 : 4 and for the roaster it is about 3 : 1. Basins and jars are both used for storage. But the former is for short term-storage and is also used to feed cattle. Therefore, the opening is much larger than that of the jar (about four times).

There can also be variation in the ratio between various parts of a pot. This is related to the way a particular pot is to be used. One may notice that rim to neck ratio of rice *handi* is less than that of the multipurpose *handi*, and the rim to height ratio of the former is more than that of the beef cooking *handi*. Variation in morphometry is sometimes area specific: the sieve for making *muri* in the north (rim = body) is different from that in the west (rim < body). The first is a proper sieve with perforations and in the second, the puffed rice is shaken out through a channel as the sand settles down. The rim to height ratio of a cattle trough is less in the west than in the south. The practice of the western districts is to stick these vessels into the ground whereas in the south it is mostly free standing.

It is usually expected that an increase in size would mean proportionate increase in all parts of the vessel. However, this is not true for the pitcher and *handi* where the neck and rim sizes stay stable but the body and height increase or for the frying pan where body and rim increase, while the height is stable. Obviously, this is because proportionate increase may compromise functional efficacy.

Therefore, to assign functions to excavated potsherds or even entire pots on the basis of proportions is not always correct. Multivariate coordinated display (described in Chapter 3) might help us to group pots and potsherds by plotting matching similar forms.

It is difficult to ascertain to what extent the manufacturing method may influence shape. Miller (1985) opined that techniques were evolved around form. A pitcher or a *handi* are partly wheel-made (the upper part) and in some cases entirely handmade. This does not have much association with shape. As Carol Kramer (1997) noticed that in Rajasthan carination is created by paddling and is not formed due to the attachment of the lower body to the upper body. I have found that carination can also be created on the wheel. The *sara,* or the offering tray, and the *tawa* for roasting roti, are convex bottomed, averaging around 7 cm. in height, and are made by dabbing the clay over a concave surface (usually a lid).

Some of the function-induced manufacturing decisions vary from region to region because of the differences in local clay. This has a bearing on fabric than on shape. While coarse grain sands are brought to South 24 Parganas all the way from the west to make vessels that can be put on fire, Birbhum potters make everything with the same clay. While fine river sand is used with dabbers in south Bengal, the western districts use ash. In both cases there will be come variation in the surface of the lower part of the pot. This would in effect increase the difference between coarse and fine vessels of southern Bengal.

Lastly, we need to explore to what extent variations are a matter of chance over conscious creation. When we look at manufacturing methods we can see that a lot of small differences that are associated with description of rim types are often produced involuntarily. Finger movements that make featureless, everted, internally thickened, or tapering rims involve very small moves and fine timing on the rotating wheel. The difference between outturned and flaring, or flaring and obliquely splayed rims is also a matter of a very few degrees.

Yet, between outturned and obliquely splayed, or flaring and horizontally splayed rims, we can surely observe the role of conscious decision. Besides, I found that same type of pitcher produced by the same potter may have a tapering neck or concave one, and a rounded shoulder or a sloping one. These differences are probably produced during attachment of the lower part to the upper body and subsequent beating with paddle and anvil.

The pottery produced by individual potters nevertheless shows a remarkable uniformity (Chapter 4). Variations were noticed only by studying the cross-section. These were noticed in the slightly more complicated forms of rim like the clubbed or collared rim. When one takes a trans-regional view one may find that for some types the variation is minimal as with the pitcher, and some forms like the *muri* sieve exhibit strong regional features.

Some items like the ritual pot show a great amount of regional variation in shape, but at the same time display strong uniformity within a smaller locality. Such variations are not adequately reflected by morphometry. Within a locality, the physical aspect acts as a functional marker for the specific type of ritual. Today the practices of Hinduism in West Bengal are associated with a broadly similar philosophy and rituals, most of these are associated with water. A constricted neck and rounded body are common to all these pots. The morphometry of these vessels is, therefore, similar. But local style is equally important as the variation in form suggests.

The variations noticed among 'secular' pots of different regions are sometimes simply local variations which may be assigned to the domain of style. The rice cooking pot generally maintains an overall similarity in shape. Malda and Birbhum have a longer range of rim size than that of Bardhaman and South 24 Parganas. The shape of the *malsa* is different at Kadubari (Malda), it has incurved collared rim. At Nastika (Birbhum) there is *malsa* for cooking which has a splayed short thickened rim and carinated body that very closely resembles the *handi*. In Bardhaman and South 24 Parganas it is a bowl with closing rim. A similar shape was noticed in material from a recent excavation at Paharpur, a medieval site in Birbhum district (excavated by me in 2007–8 with Suchira Roychoudhury and Kaushik Gangopadhyay). Open mouthed *handis* are favoured in Birbhum district and at Malda. The *muri* roasters from Bardhaman and Birbhum are similar, except for Nastika in Birbhum, which is similar to the Malda variety. At Malda the roasters have splayed rims, constricted and short necks, and globular to bulging bodies. The sieve for puffed rice is the same in Bardhaman and Birbhum. The trough for feeding cow (*patna or daba*) is the same in Bardhaman and Birbhum, and those found in South 24 Parganas and Malda are similar. The looped handled pan is similar everywhere except at Gafulia (Bardhaman), which has an externally thickened rim and at Kadubari (Malda) with slightly straightened sides.

The question of style and choice is more obvious where decoration is concerned. It could be a simple black band in case of a pitcher from Nakali which is 'necessary' for the product to sell in the local market, as a local person said. Or it could be incised decoration on pottery made for Muslims in Malda. At Mai-Bibir Hat, the local water jars have rounded bodies and red slip. Those brought to the market from Beral in Medinipur district are carinated at the waist and have black slip. Here the difference in colour does not stand in the way of selling the product.

The association of style with formal variation is common but sometimes it is also reflected in the choice of technique. Jars are manufactured with the slab technique in Ramkrishnapur in Birbhum, and a similar method is also present in Bardhaman but used for the large basin. In both cases the base is luted on later. In South 24 Parganas jars are made by joining sections made over a mould.

As for the response of the market to style, this is not uniform. The villages that were surveyed catered mostly to the local market, the manufacturing village itself, or within a 15–20 km. radius of it. The sweet shops of Kolkata look for size, not style. An earthen vessel serves as a short-term storage facility, used to transport sweets home. True, there is consumer response to style. The water pitcher and date juice pot are very similar in morphometry and even form. Therefore, one product may be mistaken for another in a different locality but not within. Style is sometimes only a matter of decoration. Without decoration a pot would not be sold in the market. In Birbhum, the pots that are made in the villages of Ajay valley have more in common with that of other pots from the same district than those of Bardhaman on the same river, which is nearer. This may be due to the market which is in Bolpur, 15–20 km. north. Bardhaman potters sell their product in Katwa, situated further east. At the same time, pottery from Medinipur district that is sold in South 24 Parganas is very different but acceptable to the local population. How far all this is related to the continuing migration of population is difficult to ascertain.

The theory that pottery is partly a product of communication between producer and user (Sheiffer and Skibo 1997) is relevant. At the very local level, the interactions probably start right in the potter's home. Even here the maker and user may not be differentiated. Many pots are made by women as much as they are mostly used by women (Appendix II).

SPATIAL MANIFESTATIONS OF VARIATION AND ITS IMPLICATION

The archaeological question behind the variations in assemblages is what has caused the variation. The answer is usually sought in culture contact. In the ethnographic context, although the data is more complete, cultural explanation may remain somewhat elusive. This is because the components or configurations of a culture at a particular point of time are themselves a product of the past. Our knowledge about even the recent past is at times fragmentary. It can only partially be explained. But why some impressions prevail over others, why certain norms are accepted and others are rejected, is difficult to ascertain.

An attempt is here made to explain formal variations through the manufacturing method followed in West Bengal and social and economic contacts between the areas and the potting communities.

It is clear from the present survey, as well as from the surveys conducted in the 1960s, that cultural behaviour is not homogenous as far as the production of pottery is concerned. The block wheel was reported to be in use in Champaran and Darbhanga districts of Bihar, Goalpara district of Assam, parts of Madhya Pradesh, Kutch and Mahesana districts in Gujarat and Malda and Birbhum in West Bengal (Saraswati and Behura 1966). The present survey did not find the block wheel in Birbhum, only at Malda. At Nakali in South 24 Parganas, the block wheel is made of cement. The pivoted spoked wheel, which is more common in West Bengal, is also found in parts of south India, Assam, Bastar in Madhya Pradesh and Akola, Chanda and Nander in Maharashtra, as far as published evidence tells us.

The baked clay anvil reported from Assam, north Bengal, north Orissa, Rajasthan, Punjab and Uttar Pradesh is in use throughout West Bengal. Again, stone anvils reported in Birbhum (Saraswati and Behura 1966) were not found in the present survey. The terracotta knobbed anvil has been reported during the exploration of Kusumjatra, in Birbhum, which has medieval and chalcolithic levels (Sharmi Chakraborty with Suchira Roychoudhury and Kaushik Gangopadhyay in 2007–8, followed by excavation in 2009–10). Therefore, it can be confirmed that use of knobbed terracotta anvil is not new to this region.

Concerning beating, the northern method prevails in the Malda region where wheel-made pots were beaten to shape, and the eastern technique in South 24 Parganas where only the lower part is attached by beating. In Birbhum, a modified version of the northern technique was observed in handmade pottery, together with the eastern technique.

In Birbhum, our present survey found the existence of the concave mould. A similar technique is noticed in Darbhanga and Champaran in Bihar. As for the convex mould, it is found in most parts of West Bengal and has been reported from Uttar Pradesh.

In the present survey we observed the use of vertical kilns (different derivations) in the western part and Malda. In the South 24 Parganas, kilns with stoke holes in the side was seen. Both types are found in Bihar, Assam, and Orissa. The latter type has also been reported in Kerala (Saraswati and Behura 1966).

It appears from the earlier discussion that Malda and Birbhum, which have shared a few stray similarities in form, have more in common in the manufacturing method. These methods are in turn similar to those used in Bihar. The South 24 Parganas follow many general trends that are common all over with a few trends prevalent in south India.

It is expected that geographically contiguous regions would share similar cultural traits. Malda's relation with the districts of Bihar goes much deeper. The potter communities of the states intermarry. It is probably the Bihar connection that explains the similarity of the traits between Malda and Birbhum. Though Birbhum shares borders with south Bihar, ties with the state are not so evident in the present as they were in the recent past. The Census report (Thomson 1923) mentions immigration in the western districts from the west in the early twentieth century and there was also a pilgrimage route from Bihar through the region to Orissa (Sanyal 2004).

The cultural contact of South 24 Parganas with Orissa is through Medinipur district. Many people of the latter region have settled in the South 24 Parganas, where, pottery from Medinipur continues to be sold in markets. However, the cultural links of this region with the region farther south goes back by 2,000 years into Early Historic period when the sites of both the regions have shown similar pottery types (Chakraborty 2000).

Birbhum and Bardhaman being contiguous districts do share many things in common. This is easily related to a common historical experience and local conditions. Yet Bardhaman and South 24 Parganas could not be directly linked. It could be the features of a past legacy that survived, or it could be fresh impressions made by immigrant potters from Bardhaman who work in Kolkata, that explain similarities.

VARIATION–CLASSIFICATION–ARCHAEOLOGICAL INTERPRETATION

From the earlier discussion we have seen that the creation of variation is a predetermined process. The varieties of earthenware created by traditional potters are socially significant shapes recognized by consumers and are known to serve specific purposes. The process of creation is transferred down the generations and it becomes a part of a mental template. This is such an internalized process that sudden innovations would be difficult. Even small changes like the creation of different shapes at a single sitting are avoided, and different sizes of the same item are usually not made. This may be partly because many pots are produced from a single throw and the girth/base of the pot depends to an extent on the diameter of the thrown clay. This creates possibility of making a certain size and shape over and over again. At the same time, it introduces rigidity akin to automated machine which stifles innovation.

In an archaeological context, this would mean that the appearance of new shapes is unlikely without a strong incentive. Disappearance of shapes would, for its part mean, a lack of demand. Partial modification of types, whether morphometric or cosmetic, would also require a certain amount of incentive. As Coomaraswamy (1979) said, 'it would not occur to the potter to work for mere amusement or for production of beautiful forms apart from practical ends'.

Therefore, the presence or absence of the multiple shapes in a particular functional form could hold the key to the understanding of the composition of population as well as communication with different groups of people. Networks and trade are often emphasized by archaeologists and historians working on Early Historic period. Convergence or difference can also reveal how cosmopolitan/heterogeneous the population was that the pottery assemblage catered to.

When we look into the variety produced locally and used locally, some finer variation come to our notice. Among pots manufactured by a single potter, differences would not be noticed quickly. Much of it was possible because analysis in this study involved the drawing of cross sections of these pots. These differences constitute normal variations produced during manufacture. As my analysis has shown, it is only a little less pressure that would make a particular vessel rim outturned and not flaring, or flaring and not obliquely splayed. A slight pressure of the fingers can make externally thickened rim concave instead of rounded. It is important, in other words, to understand what a deliberate variation is and distinguish it from the casual.

However, if one carefully considers manufacturing methods, one can distinguish broadly the shapes that should fall together in a group and those that should be apart. Miller (1985) has remarked that it is difficult to associate particular type of hand movement with a particular form. This is only partially true for forms that are remodelled at a later stage or beaten to a completely different shape. Certain deliberate hand movements are certainly responsible for certain shapes, especially those of the rims. It may be worthwhile to classify and organize these in an order of complexity based on hand movements (see Appendix I).

The previous discussion has shown that sometimes differences in morphometry would mean different functions. But in an archaeological context, such differences may escape proper classification. Indeed many of these variations might be treated as subtypes or varieties as the entire shapes may not be available.

A more intense study of morphometry might be helpful. It seems from the study of pottery from the market that size does not vary more than 2 cm. for a single group. This standard should be acceptable in archaeological contexts from the Early Historic period onwards (at least), when pottery had become a specialized craft.

This study has also tried to throw light on different kinds of size fluctuations for different shapes. For the pitcher, only body size—width and height—would increase; with the frying pan height is likely to stay stable; with the vegetable pot an increase in size would be proportionate.

Fieldwork among potters today teaches us that designation of shape according to proportions of body parts could be difficult. Even to base it on correlation of sizes of different parts may be very useful in some cases but misleading in others. This poses a question for functions that are attributed to archaeological sherds.

The ethnography of Dangwara (Miller 1985) suggests that all pots are for multiple uses as they become container vessels after sometime when they cannot perform their primary function. However, original multipurpose vessels, at least in West Bengal, are open-mouthed pots with no curve unduly emphasized. Reuse of vessel is based on maximum utilization of resource and sometimes broken vessels are further shaped to suit their present purpose.

A few general reference points may be drawn about stylistic variation associated with rim type. These constitute voluntary and involuntary variations possible within a particular type. Though the level of standardization within potting communities may vary, it might yield better result if we can club a few forms together. We may also think of conceptualizing shapes as progressively evolving (see Appendix 1). For example:

Externally thickened→clubbed→horizontally splayed→drooping

All these variations, big and small, are linked to the question of skill of the potter and the demand for the produce. This, in turn, is linked to the social context where both ethnicity and function have a role to play. Both the nature of the record and archaeological method will be a guide to handling the question.

Appendix I

Classification of Excavated Pottery

THIS ETHNOGRAPHIC STUDY of the formal variations in archaeological pottery and the possible causes of such variations, shows that how variations are present even in functionally similar pots in different regions, and in different villages of the same region (Chapters 2 and 3). Variations may emerge in vessels produced by the same potter also (Chapter 4). The differences in manufacturing process that cause these variations have also been discussed (Chapter 5).

The understanding that has emerged is now used to classify formal variations in the rim of which there is a large proportion of documented data in excavation reports. The other aim was to see if this classification could reveal any chronological pattern that may in its turn indicate change in human behaviour over time. I will organize ceramic rim varieties into groups reflecting an order of complexity of form and which requires some decision making.

Most Indian excavation reports, more specifically those of historical period, include documentation of pottery as a catalogue of finds from sites. This documentation has been extensively used by archaeologists to make cultural associations and to compare one site with other sites and/or assign them to cultures and chronology. Yet variation of form as a factor has been neglected.

Rim is a part of the pot that fulfills a purpose related to the specific use of the vessel. It also symbolizes the identity of the maker or user. The collared rims are found in large storage vessels which have to be moved by gripping the rim from top. The clubbed rims are found on the juice collecting pots which can be hung with a string tied under it. In Chapter 4 we have noted how similar the rims of pitchers made by the same potter are (Fig. 4.2). We have also observed how the rims of pitchers made by a different potter are different (Fig. 4.19). Both the products sold in the same market might fulfil the purpose of an identify marker to indicate the workshop from where the products originate. Similarly, there is little difference between water pitcher and a date juice pitcher made by the same potter except the neck is shorter and the rim different. Both forms might serve each other's purpose but these small differences designate their purpose. Therefore, there is a need to go beyond individual forms in order to understand human intentions.

In the present study the method of classification has been derived from ethnographic study of how variations are generated by the manufacturing process. This gives insight into how to distinguish intended variations from those not intended by the potter. I now attempt to create an order of development, or change in forms according to complexity. This, to an extent signifies, a level of skill and decision the potters took to execute it.

The sequences may be grouped in order of complexity as described below.

1. After centring the clay on the wheel, the both the thumbs are inserted into it and are pushed outwards increasing the girth, this makes incurved featureless rim (Pl. 5.15)
2. As the height increases, the palm of right hand supports the wall and the thumb exerts pressure on the exterior below the rim, making it thick (Pl. 5.16)
3. The right hand applies pressure on the upper part below the rim, which causes the mouth to open up and the neck to constrict, while the left hand supports the rim hinged between the index and third finger (Pl. 5.39)
4. As the right fingers are placed on the neck for support, the fingers of the left hand press the interior of the rim, and it flares out. The thumb placed on the top of the rim gives it a sharp edge (Pl. 5.40)
5. A. The fingers of the right and the left hand slide up the rim making it thinner.
   B. The thumb and first finger of the left hand are placed out and other fingers placed above the rim, drawing clay from inside and rounding up the edge of the rim making it collared (Pl. 5.24).
   B1. Then the left thumb is placed under the rim and the rest inside. The first finger of the right hand presses the rim exterior flattening the front. The rim becomes clubbed (Pl. 5.23).
6. The stem is placed horizontal at the base of the rim and the left thumb and forefinger placed across it to gently support the underside of the rim as it flares out. The left hand slowly rolls over the rim from the inner wall bending it down further. Through steady application of pressure, the rim is horizontally splayed. (Pl. 5.37).
7. Then fingers placed interior slides out and down over the stem that supports the rim from below to make the rim drooping (Pl. 5.43).

These steps are the descriptions of manufacturing processes creating vessels which are tall, like the pitcher and the jar. The potters say that they can make a vessel up to a height of a foot but presently these jars and pitches are partly made on wheel and are only about 20 cm. high. The lower part is attached separately (see p. 100, Pl. 5.8). Clubbed and collared rims are formed sometimes before and sometimes after the rims are splayed and drooping, by folding the clay on the body. But the latter was more of a corrective measure than a routine scheme. It is usually dependent on the amount of clay that has to be gathered on the tip for this purpose. The actions required to make the specific type of rim can be delayed in taller vessels as there is more time available to gather the clay for that specific form of rim.

In spite of some contradictions in the observations, an order may be perceived in terms of complexity in manufacturing process. This is because there is little possibility of manual gestures on the wheel being too different in different regions: they consist of simple gestures. There may be small changes in the order of the groups (classified below) depending on the height of the vessel on wheel. Taller vessels allow greater flexibility to incorporate or alter features. In view of the fact that the potter faced some trouble in making horizontally splayed and drooping rims, it may be argued that the processes need more skills than the clubbed rim (see pp. 136, 140). It should be stressed again that any shape that is regularly made ceases to be complex for the potter in terms of cognition and dexterity because of the readily usable template that is available and one type is continually produced in one sitting. However, individual skill is always recognized by potters and it has an impact on the overall appearance of their output.

The amount of unintended variations that are normal for non-mechanized production might vary from potter to potter. The samples that were collected from Mai-Bibir Hat in South 24 Parganas are very standardized in the case of a particular workshop. There are variations between products of different potters and some are intentionally made different.

With the manufacturing method as a guide, ceramics from excavation reports are grouped according to the rim type. The types of shapes of rim that are reported in the literature are numerous. On the basis of direction in which the rim is moving they may be grouped into internally drooping, closing, incurved, inturned, vertical, outturned, flaring, obliquely splayed, horizontally splayed and externally drooping. However, when the manufacturing technique is taken into account, the order of complexity of these groups is not the same. There are many more forms within each of these rim types. The present classification is based on the sequence of action that the potter has to take to produce a particular form. These include hand movements that displace the clay, gather the clay and shape it. The last includes special features that were added to it through the use of separate tools.

The Group T is without inflection (change in direction); it includes incurved/inturned and outcurved rim types. They are all the result of a single process of widening the mouth of pot. Group V stands for the vertical rim types. They are created by widening of the mouth and supporting the wall from both sides to an erect position. This group also includes slightly outturned rims, positioned at an angle of more than 90° and ≤ 95° from the base. The Group O has inflections and movement of the rim is outward. This group includes outturned, flaring, obliquely splayed and horizontally splayed rims. Flanged rims are distributed among T, V and O. In these rims (here it means those rims which bifurcate, a term often used in many excavation reports) clay may be drawn from the body of the pot or sometimes folded in. The internally drooping rim is found to be present only in incurved and outcurved variety, i.e. in the 'T' group, while internally folded ones are found in 'O' group.

Groups T, V and O contain subgroups denoted by a numbers 1 to 8; these signify an ascending order of complexity. This is again divided into sections such as T1a or T1b, representing formal differences not necessarily a change in skill or effort. The difference between adjacent alphabets is minimal and sometimes their position may be interchangeable. Each group formed consists of several members with both intended and unintended variations. The difference in gestures that produce each member is minimal and they share a formal resemblance. The relation among the subgroups is closer in simpler forms and becomes looser in complex forms.

It is also to be noted that some apparently simple forms, like the incurved featureless rim, when they occur in the pitcher or jar, are developed much later from a clubbed shape and, therefore, would be placed at a higher level of complexity in these forms. This is because the direction of movement of the clay in an outturned rim is outwards. The clay is accumulated at the top to thicken the rim and finally the incurved rim is made by displacing clay from inner side and rounding up the exterior or by changing the direction upwards. The ones with inflection, therefore, have been placed under group 'O' and described under 'carinated' subclass. However, some are shaped from the same sequence with the flaring out rim making it slightly outcurved and not carinated.

The groups are as follows:

1. T1a: incurved featureless/thickened/externally grooved, inturned featureless/thickened/externally grooved, outcurved featureless/thickened/grooved.

FIGURE 1: T1a

2. T1b: incurved internally thickened/inbeaded, inturned internally thickened/inbeaded, outcurved internally thickened/inbeaded

FIGURE 2: T1b

3. T1c: incurved sharpened, inturned sharpened, outcurved sharpened

FIGURE 3: T1c

4. T1d: incurved everted/everted externally carinated, outcurved everted/everted externally carinated, inturned everted

FIGURE 4: T1d

5. T2a: incurved externally beaded/rounded/bulbous, inturned externally beaded/rounded/bulbous, outcurved externally beaded/rounded/bulbous/flattish externally thickened.

FIGURE 5: T2a

6. T2b: incurved flat/bevelled/flat grooved/vertically bevelled, inturned flat/bevelled/thick flattish, outcurved flat/beveled/flat grooved

FIGURE 6: T2b

7. T2c: incurved thick externally beveled/beveled top/externally thick internally beveled, inturned thick beveled, outcurved thick beveled top/externally beveled.

FIGURE 7: T2c

8. T2d: incurved/outcurved with grooved or depressed top

FIGURE 8: T2d

9. T3a: outcurved externally thick sloping/externally grooved/internally thick sloping, incurved externally thick grooved

FIGURE 9: T3a

10. T3b: incurved internally beaked/flat internally beaked/externally thickened internally beaked/outcurved internally beaked

FIGURE 10: T3b

11. T3c: outcurved externally thick internally grooved

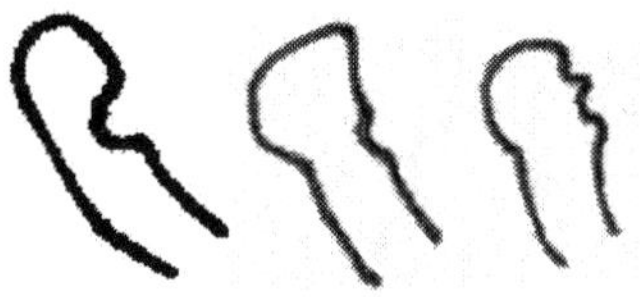

FIGURE 11: T3c

12. T3d: outcurved externally beaked/externally thickened triangular, incurved externally beaked

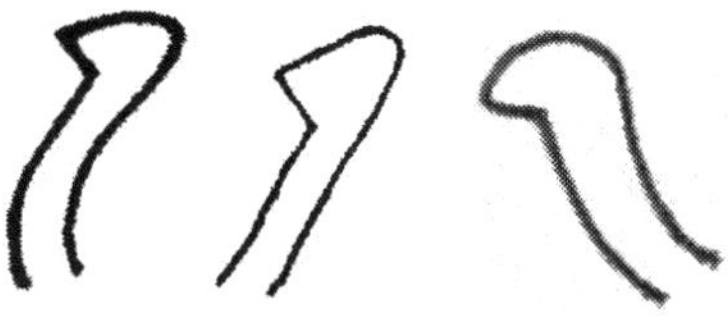

FIGURE 12: T3d

13. T3e: incurved internally thick facetted

FIGURE 13: T3e

14. T4a: outcurved externally thick, incurved externally thick/externally thick flat, incurved externally thick

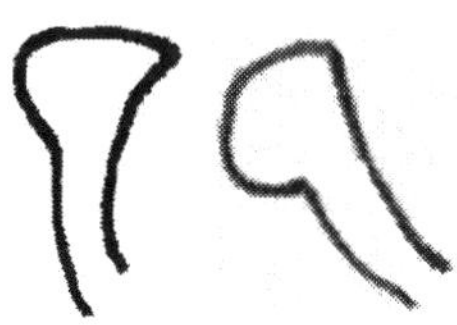

FIGURE 14: T4a

15. T4b: inturned externally beaked/clubbed triangular, incurved flat beaked/flat clubbed triangular

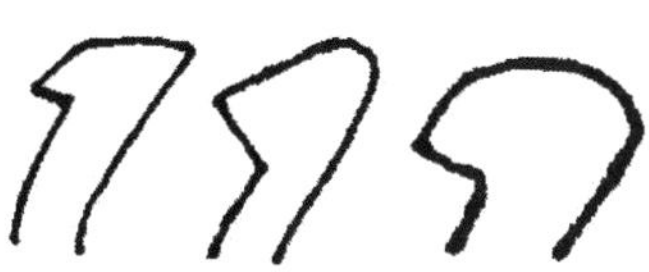

FIGURE 15: T4b

16. T4c: outcurved externally thick/externally thick sloping/collared

FIGURE 16: T4c

17. T4d: inturned externally thick with bisecting groove

FIGURE 17: T4d

18. T4e: outcurved externally thick sloping/drooping

FIGURE 18: T4e

19. T4f: outcurved externally thick sloping with ridged top

FIGURE 19: T4f

20. T4g: inturned collared/rounded/elliptical, incurved collared/rounded/elliptical, outcurved collared/rounded/elliptical

FIGURE 20: T4g

21. T4h: incurved bulbous externally beveled, outcurved bulbous externally beveled

FIGURE 21: T4h

22. T4i: outcurved externally ridged/externally ridged internally grooved, incurved externally thickened ridged, inturned externally ridged

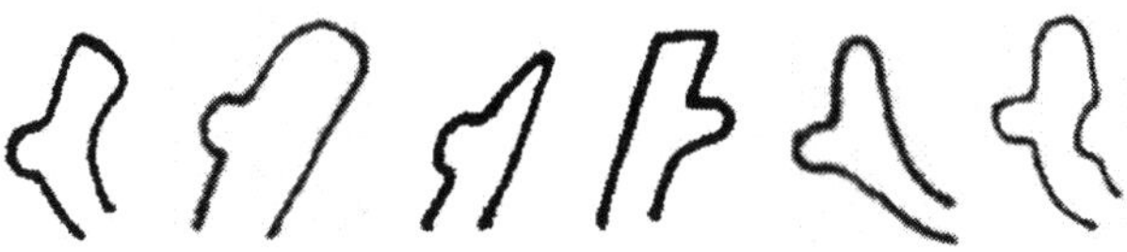

FIGURE 22: T4i

23. T4j: outcurved/incurved/inturned internally ledged

FIGURE 23: T4j

24. T5a: outcurved clubbed with bisecting groove, incurved clubbed with bisecting groove and grooved top, inturned clubbed flat with bisecting groove

FIGURE 24: T5a

25. T5b: inturned/incurved clubbed externally sloping

FIGURE 25: T5b

26. T5c: outcurved clubbed square/clubbed square internally depressed, inturned clubbed square

FIGURE 26: T5c

27. T5d: outcurved nailhead/nailhead flat with grooved top, incurved nailhead, inturned nailhead flat/inturned nailhead flat with multigrooved top

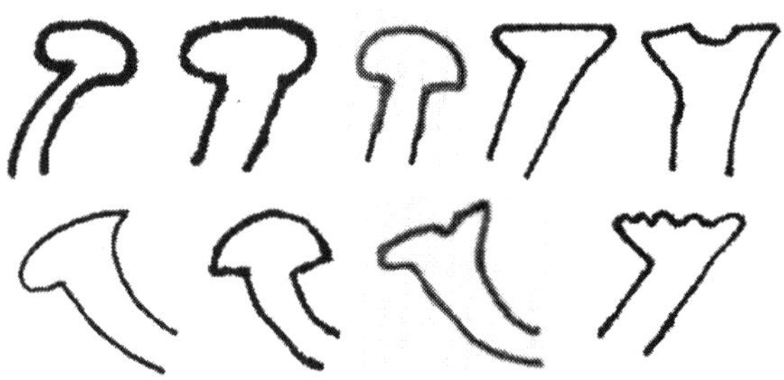

FIGURE 27: T5d

28. T5e: incurved collared rounded internally depressed/collared straight internally depressed, inturned collared, outcurved collared straight internally depressed

FIGURE 28: T5e

29. T5f: outcurved externally thick drooping/externally thick flat drooping

FIGURE 29: T5f

30. T6a: incurved collared with bisecting groove

FIGURE 30: T6a

31. T6b: incurved externally thick multigrooved/bulbuous multigrooved/flat externally thick multigrooved, inturned externally thick multigrooved, outcurved collared multigrooved.

FIGURE 31: T6b

32. T6c: incurved clubbed bisecting groove ridged top

FIGURE 32: T6c

33. T6d: outcurved short splayed

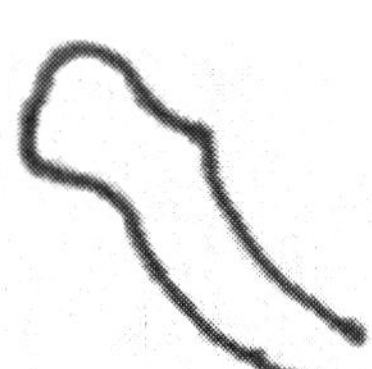

FIGURE 33: T6d

34. T6e: short splayed clubbed/clubbed with bisecting groove

FIGURE 34: T6e

35. T7a: outcurved/incurved/inturned externally ledged (or flanged)

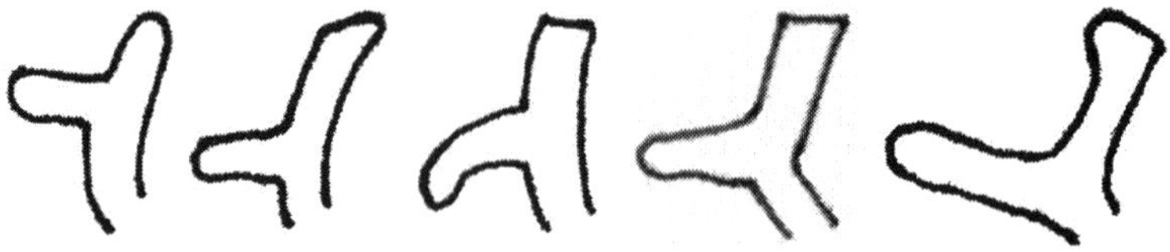

FIGURE 35: T7a

36. T7b: closing featureless

FIGURE 36: T7b

37. T8a: incurved/outcurved internally drooping

FIGURE 37: T8a

38. T8b: incurved/outcurved collared internally drooping

FIGURE 38: T8b

39. V1a: vertical featureless/sharpened/thickened, outturned featureless

FIGURE 39: V1a

40. V1b: vertical flat/thick flattened

FIGURE 40: V1b

41. V1c: vertical internally thickened/inbeaded

FIGURE 41: V1c

42. V2a: vertical externally thickened/externally thickened grooved

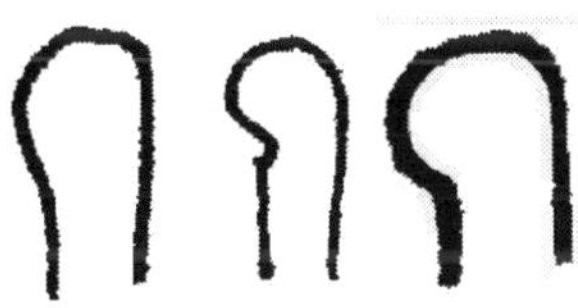

FIGURE 42: V2a

43. V2b: vertical flat grooved on top/grooved on top internally/with depression on top internally/flat externally grooved

FIGURE 43: V2b

44. V2c: vertical externally beveled/internally beveled

FIGURE 44: V2c

45. V3a: vertical externally thickened/externally thickened internally beveled/externally thick straight undercut

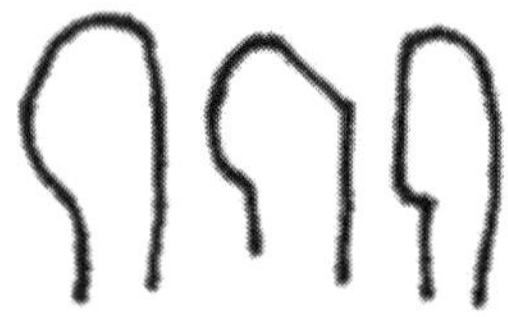

FIGURE 45: V3a

46. V3b: vertical externally thickened sloping/beaked

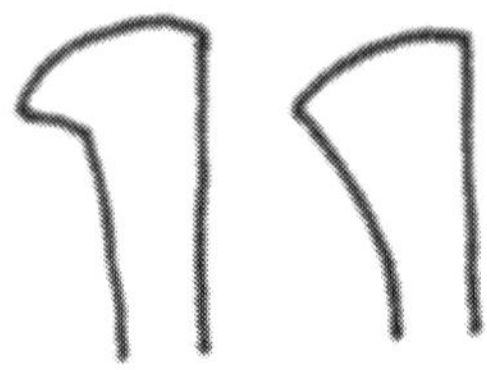

FIGURE 46: V3b

47. V3c: vertical internally beaked

FIGURE 47: V3c

48. V4a: vertical externally thick sloping/externally thick triangular

FIGURE 48: V4a

49. V4b: vertical ridged externally/ridged externally internally grooved/thick externally ridged/everted externally ridged

FIGURE 49: V4b

50. V4c: vertical collared ridged/collared everted ridged

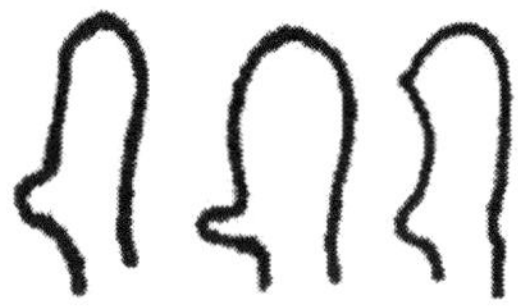

FIGURE 50: V4c

51. V5a: vertical collared/vertical collared undercut/collared rounded/bulbous pointed/collared with flat top

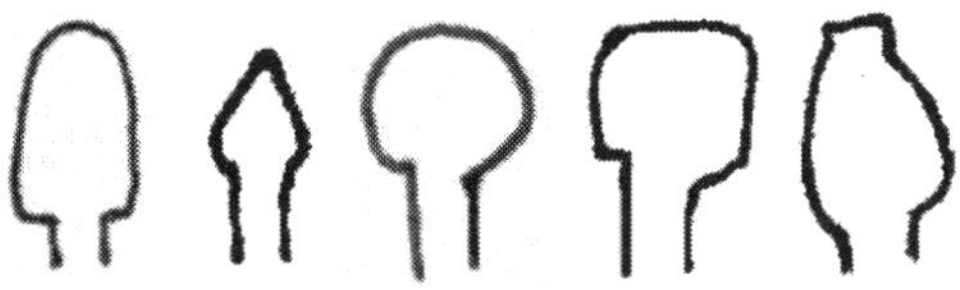

FIGURE 51: V5a

52. V5b: vertical clubbed square/clubbed square internally depressed

FIGURE 52: V5b

53. V5c: vertical clubbed concave internally grooved/square concave

FIGURE 53: V5c

54. V5d: vertical clubbed with bisecting groove/bisecting groove internally depressed

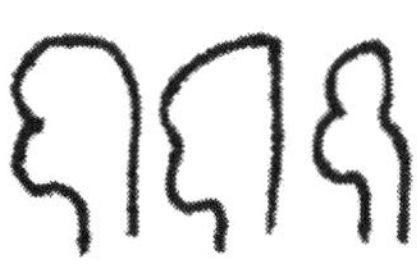

FIGURE 54: V5d

55. V5e: vertical clubbed triangular/clubbed triangular with external groove

FIGURE 55: V5e

56. V5f: vertical clubbed square with bisecting groove/bisecting groove internally depressed

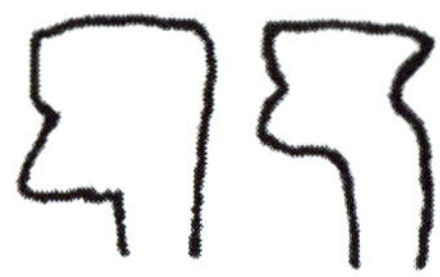

FIGURE 56: V5f

57. V5g: vertical nailhead/nailhead flat/nailhead internally depressed

FIGURE 57: V5g

58. V6a: vertical clubbed multigrooved/externally thick sloping ribbed and ledged internally grooved/collared flattish externally ribbed internally ledged

FIGURE 58: V6a

59. V6b: vertical collared with bisecting groove/ribbed internally depressed

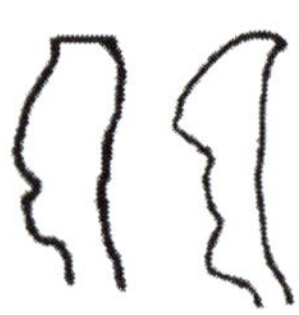

FIGURE 59: V6b

60. V6c: vertical collared elliptical/collared externally sloping notched/ collared externally sloping notched internally depressed/collared rounded internally depressed

FIGURE 60: V6c

61. V7a: vertical featureless with ledge/outturned externally thick sloping externally and internally ledged

FIGURE 61: V7a

62. O1a: outturned/featureless/sharpened, flaring featureless/sharpened/ tapering

FIGURE 62: Ola

63. O1b: outturned everted/everted internally thick/everted internally depressed/externally thickened/externally thickened with groove or depression underneath/externally thickened sloping

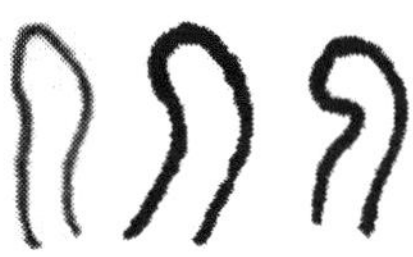

FIGURE 63: Olb

64. O1c: flaring externally grooved/internally grooved

FIGURE 64: Olc

65. O2a: flaring inbeaded/internally thickened undercut/internally thick sloping/internally thick sloping externally grooved, outturned internally thickened

FIGURE 65: O2a

66. O2b: flaring thickened/flaring bulbuous

FIGURE 66: O2b

67. O2c: flaring externally bevelled/externally bevelled internally depressed/externally sloping/internally bevelled

FIGURE 67: O2c

68. O2d: flaring flat/flat thickened/flat externally grooved/flat everted/flat depressed top

FIGURE 68: O2d

69. O3a: flaring internally beaked/flat internally thick

FIGURE 69: O3a

70. O3b: flaring flat externally thick/externally thick internally grooved

FIGURE 70: O3b

71. O3c: outturned or flaring externally thick sloping/externally thick rounded/beaded

FIGURE 71: O3c

72. O3d: outturned externally thick internally grooved

FIGURE 72: O3d

73. O3e: outturned externally thick internally depressed

FIGURE 73: O3e

74. O3f: flaring beaked/beaked internally depressed

FIGURE 74: O3f

75. O3g: flaring collared sharp

FIGURE 75: O3g

76. O4a: outturned externally thick rounded/externally thick internally pointed/externally thick internally sloping/externally thick internally beveled/flat externally rounded

FIGURE 76: O4a

77. O4b: splayed short/splayed obliquely short externally sloping

FIGURE 77: O4b

78. O4c: outturned thick drooping/drooping undercut

FIGURE 78: O4c

79. O4d: outturned/flaring collared rounded

FIGURE 79: O4d

80. O4e: outturned externally ledged/externally ledged internally grooved, flaring externally ledged

FIGURE 80: O4e

81. O4f: outturned sharp externally ledged/sharp externally ledged internally grooved/externally thick grooved ridge on top/beaked grooved ridge on top/beaked internally sharp, flaring beaked grooved ridge on top

FIGURE 81: O4f

82. O4g: flaring internally ribbed/internally ledged/externally beveled internally ledged

FIGURE 82: O4g

83. O4h: flaring externally ribbed

FIGURE 83: O4h

84. O5a: flaring clubbed/clubbed straight internally grooved, externally thick internally grooved/clubbed internally depressed

FIGURE 84: O5a

85. O5b: outturned clubbed square drooping/concave

FIGURE 85: O5b

86. O5c: outturned externally thick bisecting grooves/bisecting grooves internally grooved

FIGURE 86: O5c

87. O5d: outturned flat clubbed with bisecting groove and internally grooved/internally depressed

FIGURE 87: O5d

88. O5e: outturned clubbed square internally depressed/clubbed drooping internally depressed/clubbed externally ridged internally depressed, flaring clubbed square

FIGURE 88: O5e

89. O5f: outturned clubbed sloping

FIGURE 89: O5f

90. O5g: flaring collared with bisecting groove

FIGURE 90: O5g

91. O5h: outturned nailhead triangular/concave/rounded, flaring nailhead flat/round/flat with two grooves

FIGURE 91: O5h

92. O5i: flaring/outturned externally ledged with ridged top

FIGURE 92: O5i

93. O5j: flaring/outturned clubbed triangular

FIGURE 93: O5j

94. O5k: flaring/outturned collared

FIGURE 94: O5k

95. O6a: outturned externally thick with rib bellow/flat nailhead with ledge bellow

FIGURE 95: O6a

96. O6b: outturned short splayed clubbed/short splayed clubbed square depressed on top

FIGURE 96: O6b

97. O6c: outturned internally bulbous/internally bulbous externally ledged internally bulbous and grooved

FIGURE 97: O6c

98. O6d: splayed short depressed top/internally grooved/thickened, splayed obliquely short grooved top/thick internally ledged

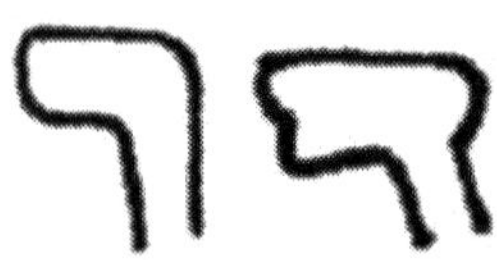

FIGURE 98: O6d

99. O6e: splayed thick sloping

FIGURE 99: O6e

100. O6f: flaring collared/collared flat

FIGURE 100: O6f

101. O6g: outturned externally thick multigrooved, flaring externally thick multigrooved/externally thick rounded multigrooved

FIGURE 101: O6g

102. O6h: outturned externally thickened flat drooping/externally thickened with bisecting grooves and drooping

FIGURE 102: O6h

103. O7a: splayed obliquely/sharp/thick/internally thick/thick sloping

FIGURE 103: O7a

104. O7b: splayed horizontally/with depressed top/pointed internally/thickened internally

FIGURE 104: O7b

105. O7c: splayed externally stepped/internally grooved/grooved top with ridge/slightly drooping with bisecting groove and ridged top

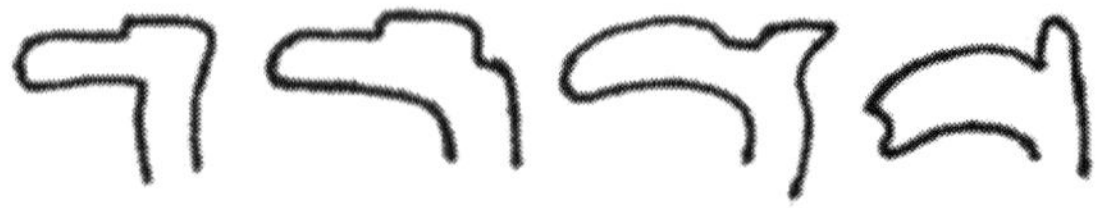

FIGURE 105: O7c

106. O7d: splayed with grooves on top

FIGURE 106: O7d

107. O7e: splayed with multigroove

FIGURE 107: O7e

108. O7f: splayed slightly drooping/slightly drooping with bisecting groove

FIGURE 108: O7f

109. O7g: carinated vertical tapering/incurved tapering/outturned tapering/vertical sharp externally rounded/vertical featureless/inturned multigrooved/vertical internally ledged/incurved externally ribbed sharpened

FIGURE 109: O7g

110. O7h: carinated externally ledged/multigrooved externally ledged/ multigrooved internally ledged, flaring carinated externally ledged, internally sharp carinated externally ribbed

FIGURE 110: O7h

111. O7i: acutely carinated/carinated with ledge

FIGURE 111: O7i

112. O7j: carinated flanged

FIGURE 112: O7j

113. O8a: flaring drooping, outturned drooping/drooping sharp/ drooping grooved top

FIGURE 113: O8a

114. O8b: thick drooping/thick drooping stepped, thick drooping internally depressed, splayed thick drooping

FIGURE 114: O8b

115. O8c: outturved drooping internally ledged/with ridged top

FIGURE 115: O8c

116. O8d: outturned internally folded

FIGURE 116: O8d

It can be understood from the above classification based on manufacturing process that the features are formed gradually, one evolving out of another, and they are not mutually exclusive. But the decision to make a particular form is usually taken before the process begins. The rim of the vessels, whether it is incurved, vertical or outturned is result of a specific effort. Within each of these groups the subgroups numbering 1 to 8 are created, signifying the ascending order of time and effort within their group. However, as mentioned earlier, there would be some shift in the effort range if height factor of the vessel type is considered. Within these subgroups further division of a, b, c, etc., are made which are caused by subtle changes in manipulation, but difficult to measure in terms of effort. For example, the third order groups like that of O7c and O7h which are formed by very different gestures but one cannot considered to be more skilled than the other. The individual forms within the subgroups may or may not be formed due to conscious decision.

Cultural Implications of this Classification

To see if this classification has implications for the interpretation of the archaeological record, the distribution of these groups were studied over a period of time. The sites that have been selected are of the period 600 BC–AD 500 but many are preceded by Chalcolithic or Early Iron Age and many continue later in to medieval period. The choice of the period is based partly on the fact that many of these sites have stratigraphic continuity to the modern period.

The chronology that is provided in the graphs is based on the excavation reports of the sites under consideration. These are Bhir Mound

(Khan et al. 2002) and Sirkap (Ghosh 1947–48) in Taxila, Ahichchhatra (Ghosh and Panigrahi 1946), Atranjikhera (Gaur 1986), Sonkh (Hartel 1993), Hastinapura (Lal 1973), Narhan (Singh 1995), Rajghat (Narain and Roy 1977), Pataliputra (Sinha and Narain 1970), Kumrahar (Altekar and Mishra 1959), Vaishali (Sinha and Roy 1969 and Deva and Mishra 1961), Sonpur (Sinha and Verma 1977), Nagda (Banerjee 1986), Navdatoli and Maheshwar (Sankalia et al. 1958), Nevasa (Sankalia et al. 1960), Ter (Chapekar 1969), Pauni (Nath 1998), Tripuri (Dikshit 1955), Veerapuram (Sastri et al. 1984), Nagarjunakonda (Khare 2006), Satanikota (Ghosh 1986), Urayur (Raman 1988) and Arikamedu (Wheeler 1946). The total number of sites is 23.

The periodization in these excavation reports is not uniform. A certain amount of simplification was required to analyse the material on similar terms. First, all the dates had to be transformed to Before Present (BP) starting with the calendar year 2000. This is to take out BC and AD and make the timeline continuous. The year 2000 has nothing to do with carbon dates. Most of the sites in the list presented earlier are excavated after 1950. The sites which record late historical pottery are very few and most of them record the end of the last phase as around 200 years from the date of excavation. The calendar year 2000 is near the latest excavation reports that are consulted here and more convenient. Second, a chronological frame like sixth century BC to second century BC, often considered the chronological span of NBPW (Northern Black Polish Ware) has been transformed into 600–200 BC, which is not exactly the same. This is done on the basis that many of the sites of the same region with similar cultural assemblage have been dated so. The upper and late phases of these periods are separated by dividing into two which is also not accurate. The aim here is more to generalize and look at a trend than present hard facts.

To make the features compact, the years were converted into phases which broadly follow cultural chronology. These are Phase 1 (3400–3000 BP) coinciding with Chalcolithic, Phase 2 (3000–2600 BP) with Early Iron Age, Phase 3 (2600–2200 BP) is early phase of Early Historic, Phase 4 (2200–1700 BP) is middle phase of Early Historic, Phase 5 (1700—1400 BP) is late phase of Early Historic, Phase 6 (1400–800 BP) is Early Medieval and Phase 7 (800–200 BP) Medieval.

We begin with the larger vessels where the potter has more time to decide, improvise and make corrections and then go on to those which would be little more than reflex action. Therefore, the taller vessel types have possibility of more complex shapes and more variation. This also means that complexity would be perceived differently in making higher and lower types.

The excavation reports do not mention how many examples of a shape were recovered. It is just the variations in shape which are recorded and sometimes different sizes are also noted. Therefore, these are basically presence and absence data. To compare between different sample sizes the bar graphs are expressed as percentages. The numbers suggests that a particular group is represented in number of specimens from one or more sites which may indicate its popularity.

Analysis

To begin from the tallest of the vessel types, the jar, the manufacturing process is most flexible. Based on the present conditions it may be about 30 cm. high. A longer time on the wheel would involve greater opportunity to enact change. Therefore, possibility for variation is much more. But many of these vessels were and are usually only partly made on wheels. Jars have a large presence in the early historic period but show a sharp peak during the early medieval. In Figure 11.7, the rim types were condensed in order of complexity into three groups. Group 1: 1–3 of T (very few, possibly a variant of similar forms in O), V and O (most represented) shows the simplest of forms to the start of the accumulation of clay in the rim, Group 2: 4–6 the clay component gradually increasing and are given distinct forms which have functional implication as well. Group 3: 7–8 are groups with complex inflections.

The graph (Fig. 117) shows a decline of Group 1 from Phase 1, as Group 2 rises in frequency from a little more than 20 to almost 70 per cent in Phase 3. Group 3 almost absent in Phase 2 is about 10 per cent or a little more in the early historic phase and increases to more than 30 per cent in the early medieval period.

Pitchers are smaller than jars but stand on an equal ground on time taken to shape them on the wheel. They are also partly manufactured by hand. But they have longer necks and the inflection is more gradual. There is no case from Phase 7, therefore it is not represented. The ordering of the groups is similar to that of the jar.

The graph (Fig. 118) shows that simpler forms do not have much presence. Group 1 which is 20 per cent in Phase 1 reduces to about 10 per cent in Phase 2 and increases very little in the subsequent phases. Group 2 is absent in Phase 1, but forms about 85 per cent of the Phase 2 types and then is less than 40 per cent in Phase 6. Group 3 is 80 per cent in Phase 1, but very scarce in Phase 2, and slowly rising to half in Phase 6.

The height of the *handi* is lower than jars and pitchers and would stand at 10–15 cm. on wheel. The diameter of the centred clay is large (about 20 cm.) and even after the mouth is widened it maintained a constriction

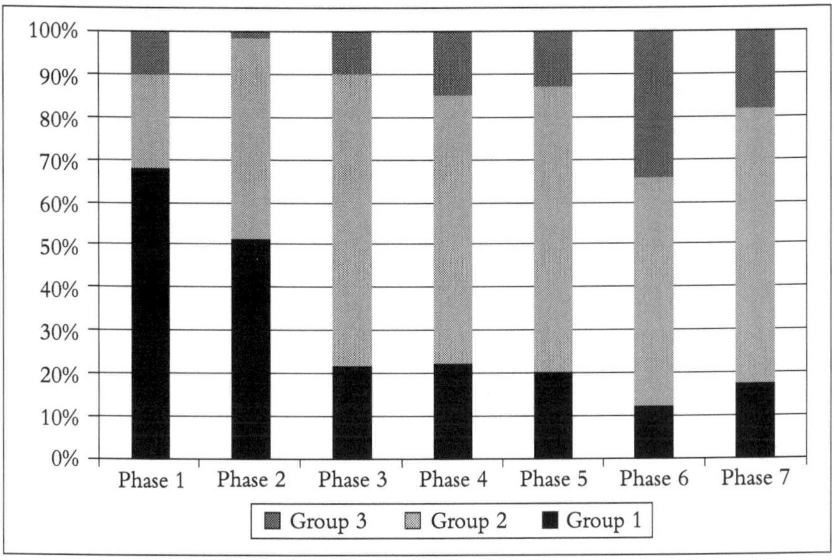

FIGURE 117: Percentage graph of groups of jar rims

at neck (see Chapter 5). But the division of groups is similar to those of the jar and the pitcher keeping in mind the similarity in manufacturing sequence. But Phase 3 has *handis* with closing featureless rim which is typical of that period. As the shape suggests, they are manufactured differently. It is

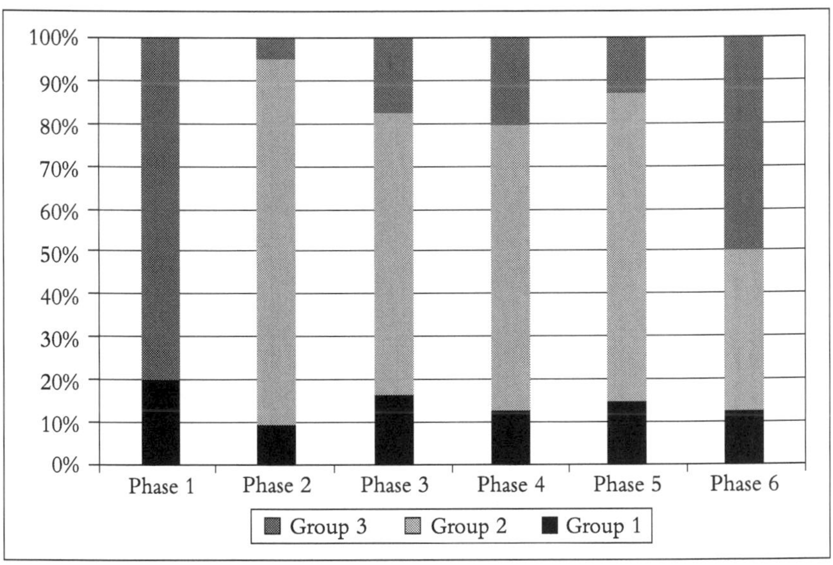

FIGURE 118: percentage graph of pitchers

shaped possibly by paddle and anvil right after opening of the mouth. Therefore these closing rims are clubbed with T1a.

The graph (Fig. 119) shows the presence of simpler forms in the early phases and increases to over 60 per cent in Phase 3 then declines. Group 3 increases its presence from Phase 3–6. Group 2 is most prominent in Phase 7.

The basin has a wide open mouth. The height of this vessel is in many cases less than *handi*. Therefore, there is less flexible in technique as there is less time. It is also a multipurpose type. It is used in serving, storage, food processing but not for cooking. Therefore, it might include a wider range of rim types. This means that the technical decisions are executed early. Therefore, accumulation of clay is not gradually done with the evolution of shape as in the case of taller forms but initiated in one go in step 2 mentioned above (also see Chapter 5) and the girth is increased later. Therefore, collared rims would be mostly early together with externally thickened varieties (Group 1) followed by the clubbed (Group 2) and the splayed and drooping types (Group 3).

Figure 120 shows that the Group 1 dominates over all the phases except Phase 5. The sample size of that period is low. But one may notice in this shape an increase in Group 3 from Phase 3. The general predominance of Group 1 with simple and collared forms largely confirms the utility of the vessels.

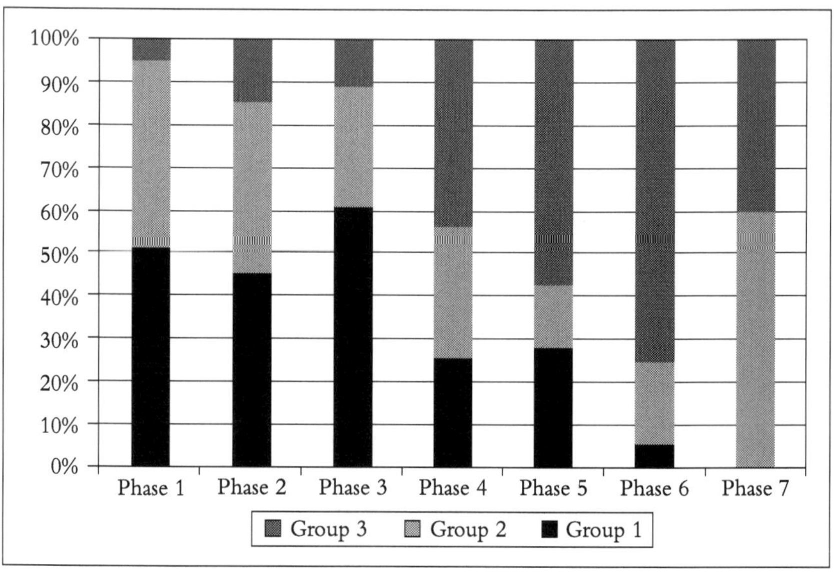

FIGURE 119: Percentage graph of *handis*

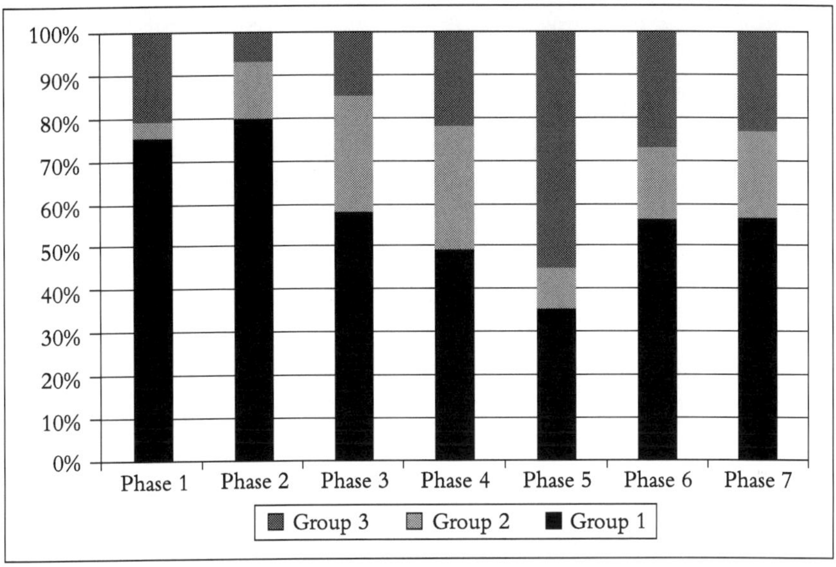

FIGURE 120: Percentage graph of basins

The bowl is a smaller, eating vessel. Complex rim forms are only a matter of stylistic preference. Here Group 1 includes only 1 and 2 of O, T and V groups. Since the height is usually low and these are open-mouthed flaring, vertical rim can be achieved in one movement. Unlike the basin, collared forms are not important. The complex forms are a matter of choice. Simpler rim forms predominate as it is evident from Figure 120. It is also chronologically restricted as most of the samples come from early historic horizon.

Figure 121 shows the preponderance of Group 1 in all phases. In Phase 6 proportion of Group 3 is almost 30 per cent. There are only two cases from Phase 7 and both belong to Group 3. There is an increase in this group from Phase 4 onwards.

The last category is the dish (Fig. 122) which is the lowest in height, ranging between 4 and 6 cm. Here almost everything would be reflex action. Complex forms would, therefore, be well thought out and tried beforehand for proper execution. The complex forms are a matter of stylistic choice. The division into groups is similar to those of the bowl. Most of the rims belong to incurved varieties which are fashioned in a single movement as the mouth of the vessel is opened up.

Figure 122 again shows that the simpler forms dominate. Group 2 is present in all the phases except Phase 6. There is only one case from Phase 5, therefore it is not represented in the graph and none in the Phase 7. Group 3 is very prominent in Phase 6.

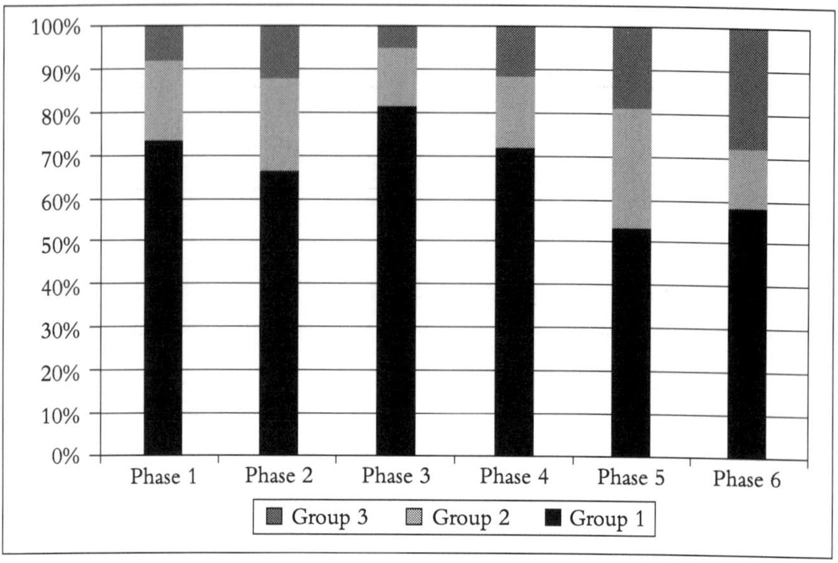

FIGURE 121: Bar graph of bowl rims

In Chapter 5 we have also noticed that the potter faced some difficulty in making a groove on the rim. But it appears from the excavation reports that the percentage of grooved rims remained stable from Phase 1 to 7. This may not have any significance. No regional preference for any of the groups was noticed either.

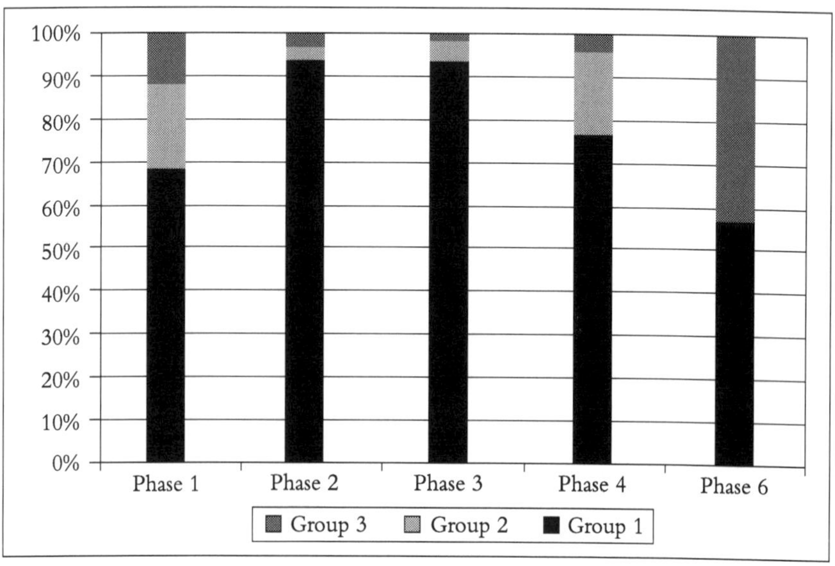

FIGURE 122: Percentage graph of dish rims

CONCLUSION

In this study I have tried to trace the pattern of rim types manufactured over chrono-cultural phases. Chalcolithic sites saw very elaborate forms of wheel-made pottery, but this discussion does not involve those samples. It neither traces the development of pottery on wheel from the earliest times. But the impact of early beginning and development can be felt in the early cultural phases of sites predominantly in of the western, north-western part of India where complex varieties are found in Phase 1(3400–3000 BP). The complex rim types from these sites contributed to the presence of complex forms in this early phase that we see in the graphs. The techniques were perhaps never lost and continue into later phase. It is noticed in the graphs above that Early Iron Age is usually associated with simpler rim types. The trend changed in the early historic phase and definitely by Phase 4 (2200–1700 BP) when complex forms increase. This change is more prominent in taller vessel types than smaller table wares.

Though never totally absent, Group 3, represented by pot forms with prominent inflections like the splayed and drooping rims, shows a general increase in the later phases. Much of it may be associated with stylistic choice as most of the glazed wares of the medieval period tend to copy porcelain table wares. This trend may be noticed in jars and pitchers also, and the coarser forms of table wares continue to have simple rim types. There is a gradual decline in the simpler forms in large vessel types except the basin. But here the sequence of steps followed in manufacturing is different. While the pot is on wheel, the thickening of the rim is almost completed before the height and the body of the vessel are increased.

What is evident is a gradual movement from the use of simple to complex forms. But does that indicate an increase in the skill of potters? It has been discussed in Chapter 5 that potters face some difficulty in manufacturing unknown shapes and prefer to continue doing the same thing. This suggests that it was changes in demand for certain types of pottery that potters adjusted their techniques so far as hand gestures on wheel are concerned.

It is interesting to note that Group 3 (consisting subgroups 7 and 8 of T, V and O) is never absent from the assemblage. It is reduced markedly in the Iron Age (Phase 2: 3000–2600 BP) but increases steadily and forms an important proportion of the assemblage. Therefore, it may be surmised that the technique of making was known but over the time it was used in all the forms discussed above in an increased number. This does reflect an increase in skill. Because it was not suddenly introduced it cannot be attributed to a sudden incentive. Nor is it a functional requirement of all the pottery types they are found. This skill might have evolved out of the greater variety of shapes that were generated in early historic phase. There was a lot of experimentation with forms in Phase 4 (2200–1700 BP). This is suggested by increasing quantity of externally thickened, collared, clubbed, horizontally splayed and flanged rim types. This process of making more complicated forms probably resulted in a generation of skills. This production of complex form was certainly sustained by a strong demand over large area of the subcontinent. This is in contrast to the concentration of Group 3 from Phase 1 (3400–3000 BP) in western and north-western India.

The classification of rim types based on order of complexity on wheel, therefore, allows a rim sherd to be considered more than a form. It is a product of human behaviour. It is a result of certain decisions and the execution of these decision depended upon skill. This method not only allowed to bring together and organize a large number of shapes but lends meaning beyond style and basic function.

Appendix II

Handmade Pots: Women in Potter's Household

POTTERY IS USUALLY associated with full time potters, men who work on the wheel. This image is very powerfully ingrained in the Indian imagination and its material foundation too is strong. Throughout India wheel-made production is practised, except in parts of the north-east.

It is now well known, however, that pottery in contemporary Indian villages is manufactured on the wheel, the wheel in conjunction with forming by hand, in the mould, and completely by hand. We are also aware that pottery, especially from the Neolithic period, was handmade. But this did not have much impact on the perception of pottery as a wheel-turned product.

This short chapter aims at drawing attention to the problems of gendered ideation of pottery manufacture and its association with wheel-made production.

Literature and Women Potters

In most ethnographies that discuss pottery manufacture, the wheel turning has been associated with men's work. In fact, no traditional wheel throwing of pots is done by women in India. However, it is noticed that kneeding and wedging the clay are done by women. They are also known to apply slip and do the artistic decoration.

The survey of twenty-seven villages incorporated a wide variety of handmade and mould-made pots. But most of the existing literature including that of Saraswati and Behura (1966), failed to mention that a significant part of these wares are made by the women of the potting household. Carol Kramer (1997) is one of the few who noted the participation of women in actual pottery production in Rajasthan.

It was found that in West Bengal, when there is an absence of male potters in some households due to death or a change in occupation, women have taken their place. In these cases, as is the practice in the rest of India, women do not use the wheel. However, in Tamil Nadu, V. Selvakumar's survey near Tanjavur (2013) has shown some women working on a wheel but not a traditional one. In many households of West Bengal both men and women were found to produce handmade pottery. Men usually make the heavier vessels and use the wheel sparsely.

It is imperative to consider whether the active participation of women in pot making is a new phenomenon. With industrialization, landless populations of the villages have migrated to towns as labourers. In general, pottery consumption has become less and there are villages where potters work as part-time farm hands.

Ancient references to potters are few. The *Vinayapitaka* (Horner 1990) mentions pottery making as lowly work, the potter supplying begging bowls to the monastery. The Jatakas also mention Bodhisattva, born as a potter, took care of his wife and children by manufacturing and selling pottery (Cowell 1990: No. 408). In another Jataka, a Bodhisattva takes shelter in a potter's house as his apprentice and turnes the wheel (Cowell 1990: No. 546). There is no mention of any productive activity by women.

Yet in the Census of India 1921 (Thomson 1923), a district-wise division is made of potters engaged full-time and those for whom it is a subsidiary occupation, with a further distinction of male and female. According to the list, full time women potters were fewer than full-time men potters in most districts. But the proportion was found to be sizeable in Burdwan (presently Bardhaman) Dacca, Malda, Murshidabad, and Dinajpur (Table 1). Though no further description of their work is available, the difference in proportion of male and female suggests that the count was taken of actual full-time pottery making and not of general assistance.

Manual Mode in Manufacture and Gender Demarcations

In the region I surveyed I found that jar and basins are made by hand, usually by men. These are large vessels whose height can go up to a metre or more in case of jar and the rim diameter would be usually above 40 cm. in case of basin. The large jar is made in parts—base, body, shoulder and rim (may also be made on wheel)—separately and each section may consist of more than one strip. These are attached by paddle and dabber and beaten to the desired shape. Only in one village was the slab method used. The body of the basin is made on a mould and the rim is hand formed and attached separately.

In contrast to this, women of the potting household make vessels for puffed rice, ritual bowls, frying pans, offering trays and lids, small basins, rice handis and occasionally water pitchers too. The height or the diameters of these vessels do not go beyond 40 cm.

Many of these vessels, like the shallow pan or tray, may start from a round lump of clay on a flat anvil, and are slowly beaten to desired

TABLE 1: Distribution of potters in Bengal in 1921
(Census Report 1923)

Principal occupation		*Susidiary occupation*		
male	*female*	*male*	*female*	*District*
331	239	244	30	Burdwan
164	56	74	5	Birbhum
4748	351	213	7	24 Parganas
103	29	17	–	Calcutta
2464	956	179	69	Dacca
34	–	3	–	Dacca city
9	–	–	–	Sikkim
710	424	20	11	Malda
688	39	196	–	Bogra
2455	443	313	38	Pabna
3904	581	105	25	Jessore
1191	660	323	28	Murshidabad
527	353	127	2	Dinajpur
463	28	44	1	Jalpaiguri
927	238	391	17	Bankura
1541	174	582	21	Medinipur

shape with help of a dabber. Sometimes a small lid would be used under a partially made vessel and turned by hand, acting as a kind of turntable-cum-mould. An anvil is used to press the clay and increase the girth of the vessel. Concave moulds that are built in the mud floor of the workshop of the potters' home are mostly used by women for making medium size vessels.

It is not always that open-mouthed vessels serve as moulds. Sometimes close-mouthed vessels are turned upside down to work as convex moulds. These are also used by women to make pots like the ritual bowl (*malsa*). The clay is spread on the surface with a concave-ended paddle or even patted down by hand. The convex moulds are mud humps built on the workshop floor or courtyard. The women of the household may do some initial work or make a small basin, but usually men work on it.

Role of the Children in Production Process

The role of the children of the household workshop is not uniform. In the villages surveyed in the South 24 Parganas, boys start helping from the age of eight years. It starts as play with boys jumping on the clay piles initiating the preparation of clay. Then, at a later stage, they help in applying slip on the pot and thereafter slowly start making handmade items, first small objects and later large objects. The initiation to the wheel usually takes place around the age of sixteen. The daughters are not involved in the production. Like most other castes of India, the Kumbhakars (or potter caste) are endogamous and the daughters' participation in production starts earnestly only when they start staying with their in-laws after marriage. But being a part of the paternal household they do take some part in production even before marriage.

In contrast, in Malda district, a toddler was observed making a clay lamp with a small dabber beside her grandmother. The lamps she manufactured will not go to the market. But her six year old sister, according to her grandmother, now makes very good lamp. Here it was found that older women are more involved in pottery making than their daughters-in-law who were busy with other household activities. In Birbhum a teenage girl was seen attending to the village shop right at the doorstep while her mother made the pot.

In South 24 Parganas, usually about 60 per cent of the products that are placed on the family kiln for firing are manufactured by the women and çhildren of the household (according to a local informant). Even if this is an overstatement, it may be surmised that manufacturing by women and children is quite substantial.

Archaeological Pottery and Gender

It is almost impossible to ascertain the role of women in the manufacture of pottery from archaeological contexts. Only a few pot sherds would yield finger prints which would show who handled the wet pot and not necessarily who made it. Ancient literature is silent about the role of women. It is safe to assume that pottery was usually manufactured in households as that is mostly the system of production mentioned in the texts. It is, thus, most probable that it was the men who worked on the wheel.

What can be done with a more careful contextual observation and classification has not been initiated by excavators as yet. This is because the role of gender has never been a concern for the excavators. Usually crudely made pots are associated with manual production and smooth and sophisticated one with the wheel. But the analyses of the handmade pots from present villages reveal that these are equally well made. There are hardly any apparent differences between handmade *handi* or pitcher and a wheel-made one. (It needs to be stressed that many wheel-made pots are only partly wheel-made.) This similarity was brought to the notice of archaeological community way back by S.P. Gupta (1968–69) who urged that sherds be observed under microscope. Allchin noticed a similarity between shapes made by potters in Mangalore by hand and some Chalcolithic and early historic shapes (1976) and remarked that many of the so called wheel-made pot actually could have been handmade. It can be strongly suggested that all round bottom vessels are at least partly handmade because wheel-made pots will have a flat base.

The problem is to devise a method to ascertain the role of women in making of the handmade pots. The survey undertaken has shown that wheel manufacturing has fallen due to a fall in demand for pottery and some types that were otherwise produced on the wheel are now made by hand. But these changes were facilitated by an existing parallel tradition of handmade pottery that is practised by women. The production process of handmade pottery already had a set of tools and techniques with which wheel-made shapes could be produced without any distinctive compromise. There is a possibility that they coexisted and predated the wheel-made versions.

If one goes by Gordon Childe's theory (1942: 67), women were the first pottery makers and these were handmade pots. This tradition never died out but was subsumed under wheel-made production as the use increased and diversified.

Communication between the producer and user is important. The emergence of distinctive shapes (Sheiffer and Skibo 1997) could result from an intricate network—between the individual producer in the household, the community and the market. Women's interactions with the majority of the products are much more intimate than those of either children or men. With most of the products being related to household work like cooking and storage, the 'market' starts at home. Many of the pots that are produced today in the Bengal village are made by the women and for women. The Census report of 1923, we have seen, shows a substantial presence of female potters. The position could have been similar in past, with continuous communication and interaction, different shapes and techniques being adapted into changing social and economic situations.

Negotiating Gender Roles in Society

In households, where the power wheel has substituted the manual, it is still the men who work on the wheel. This may be explained as that is how tradition is, but in many villages where men have left the traditional craft, women have taken over production, but still have only produced handmade pots including shapes that are traditionally made on the wheel.

The institutionalization of the process, as with many other things in India, is symbolized through rituals. This phenomenon was observed in South 24 Parganas on the day of *Chaitra Sankranti* (roughly falling on

14th of April) when work on the wheel is stopped for a month. This is traditionally the beginning of the driest month. From practical point of view, the production of pottery during this time could be more difficult due to the fast drying of clay, which might result in more breakage. The day of *Chaitra Sankranti* is an auspicious day dedicated to Shiva. It is celebrated in Bengal by pouring water on the head of *Linga* accompanied by a fair in which devotees (usually male) perform acts of self mortification. On that day the potter will shape a *linga* on wheel and lift by a thread. This is the last act before stopping the production for the month.

However, at present there are a few more acts to follow. According to my local informant (Mr Debisankar Middhya) they are much recent phenomena. The *linga* is worshipped with vermilion by potter's wife along with the household deities every day for a month. On an odd day of the month of Jayishtha (which follows the month of Baishakh in the Bengali calendar when wheel is not in use), preferably on a Saturday if not a Tuesday, two crude images are made; one of Baneswar Siva and one of Jayadurga. They are placed on the wheel. The names of the forms suggest a warrior divine couple, but who have nothing to do with pottery. They are worshipped by a brahmin priest. After worshipping the icons on wheel the priest worships Brahma as the creator god in the kiln. Here no icon is involved. On the next day all are immersed in the pond or river.

Through this ritual one may notice several social forces negotiating their roles within the small space of the potter's workshop. These include the role of the man of the family and his right over the wheel, the process of brahmanization of a rural mode of parallel worship, and ultimately the integration of the woman of the house in the process. The introduction of Jayadurga may be associated with the rising popularity of the mother goddess and impact of the Durga Puja celebrations in Kolkata which is not very far. In allowing women to play some role in the ritual process, their contributions in the household workshop is also acknowledged.

Bibliography

Alchin, F.R., 'Archaeological Significance of a Modern Indian Potter's Technique: History and Society', in *Essays in Honour of Professor Nihar Ranjan Ray*, ed. Debiprasad Chattopadhyay, Calcutta: K.P. Bagchi & Co., 1978, pp. 1–14.

Altekar, A.S. and V. Mishra, *Report on Kumrahar Excavation 1951–55*, Patna: K.P. Jayaswal Research Institute, 1959.

Arnold, Philips J. III, 'Back to Basic: The Middle Range Program as Pragmatic Archaeology', in *Essential Tensions in Archaeological Method and Theory*, ed. Todd L. VanPool and Christine S. VanPool, Salt Lake City: The University of Utah Press, 2003.

Bala, Renu, 'Ethnography and Archaeology: A Case Study of Earthen Ware', in *Ancient Ceramics: Historical Enquiries & Scientific Approach*, ed. P.C. Pant and Vidula Jayaswal, Delhi: Agam Kala Prakashan, 1997, pp. 157–76.

Banerjee, N.R., *Nagda 1955–57, Memoirs of Archaeological Survey of India*, no. 85, New Delhi: Archaeological Survey of India, Government of India, 1986.

Bhagat, Sonia, 'A Study of the Harappan Pottery Tradition in Saurashtra (with special reference to Padri and Tarasara, Bhavnagar District, Gujarat)', unpublished Ph.D. thesis, University of Pune, 2001.

Bhandarkar, D.R., *The Archaeological Remains and Excavation at Nagri, Memoirs of Archaeological Survey of India*, no. 4, Calcutta: Superintendent Government Printing Press, 1920.

Binford, Lewis R., 'Archaeology as Anthropology', *American Antiquity*, vol. 30, no. 2, pt. 1, October 1962, pp. 203–10.

Binford, Lewis R., 'Archaeological Systematics and the Study of Culture Process', *American Antiquity*, vol. 28, no. 2, pt. 2, October 1965, pp. 217–25.

Bose, N.K., 'Forward', written by Nab Kishore Behura and Baidyanath Saraswati, *Pottery Techniques in Peasant India*, Calcutta: Anthropological Survey of India, 1966.

Chakraborty, Sharmi, 'Chandraketugarh: A Cultural and Archaeological Study (thesis abstract)', *Bulletin of Deccan College P.G. and Research Institute*, vol. 60–61, 2000–1, pp. 483–8.

Chaudhuri, Sashi Bhusan et al., *West Bengal District Gazetteers: Bardhaman*, Calcutta: West Bengal District Gazetteers, 1994.

Chapekar, B.N., *Report on the Excavation at Ter (1958)*, Poona, 1969.

Childe, V. Gordon, *New Light on Most Ancient East*, Routledge and Kegan Paul Ltd., 1928; revd. edn. 1957; repr. 1964.

Childe, V. Gordon, *What Happened in History*, Harmondsworth, 1942; repr., Pelican Books, 1957.

———, *Man Makes Himself*, London: Watts, 1936.

Choski, Archana, 'Ceramic Vessels: Their Role in Illuminates Past and Present Social and Economic Relationships', *Man and Environment*, vol. XX, no. 1, pp. 87–108.

Conkey, Margaret W., 'Experimenting with Style in Archaeology: Some Historical and Theoretical Issues', in *The Use of Style in Archaeology*, ed. Margaret W. Conkey and Christine A. Hastorf, Cambridge University Press, 1990, pp. 5–17.

Coomaraswamy, Ananda K., *Medieval Sinhalese Art*, New York: Pantheon Books 1908; repr. 1979.

Cowell, E.B., *The Jataka or the Stories of the Buddha's Former Births*, Oxford: Pali Text Society, 1895; repr. 1990.

Dales, George F. and Jonathan Mark Kenoyer, *Excavation at Mohenjodaro, Pakistan: The Pottery*, University Museum Monograph 53, Philadelphia: University of Pennsylvania, 1986.

David, Nikolas and Carol Kramer, *Ethnoarchaeology in Action,* Cambridge: Cambridge University Press, 2001.

De, Barun, *West Bengal District Gazetteers: 24 Parganas*, 1994.

Deva, Krishna and V. Misra, *Vaisali Excavation*, Vaisali: Vaisali Sangh, 1961.

Dikshit, M.G., *Tripuri 1952: Being the Account of the Excavation at Tripuri*, Bhopal: Government of Madhya Pradesh, 1955.

Dunnell, Robert C., 'Style and Function:A Fundamental Dicotomy', *American Antiquity*, vol. 43, no. 2, 1980, pp. 192–202.

Gaur, R.C., *Excavation at Atranjikhera: Early Civilization in Ganga Basin*, New Delhi: Motilal Banarsidass, 1986.

Ghosh, N.C., *Excavations at Satanikota 1977–80, Memoirs of Archaeological Survey of India*, no. 82, New Delhi: Archaeological Survey of India, 1986.

Ghosh, A. and K.C. Panigrahi, 'The Pottery of Ahichchhatra, District Bareilly, UP', *Ancient India,* no. 1, 1946, pp. 37–59.

Ghosh, A., 'Taxila (Sirkap), 1944–5', *Ancient India*, vol. 4, 1947–8, pp. 41–90.

Ghosh, Dipankar, *Pashchimbanger Mritshilpa*, Kolkata: Lok Sanskriti O Adivasi Sanskriti Kendra (Department of Information & Cultural Affairs, Government of West Bengal), 2002.

Grifford, James C., 'The Type-Variety Method of Ceramic Classification as an Indicator of Cultural Phenomena', *American Antiquity*, vol. 25, no. 3, 1960, pp. 341–7.

Gupta, S.P., 'Determining the Technique of Handmade and Wheel-Turned Pottery by Microscopic Analysis', *Puratattva*, no. 2, 1968–9, pp. 23–5.

Hartel, Herbert, *Excavations at Sonkh: 2500 Years of a Town in Mathura District*, Berlin: Dietrich Reimer Verlag, 1993.

Hodder, I., *Symbols in Action: Ethnoarchaeological Studies of Material Culture*, Cambridge: Cambridge University Press, 1982.

———, *Reading the Past: Current Approaches to Interpretation in Archaeology*, Cambridge: Cambridge University Press, 1986.

———, 'Style as Historical Quality', in *Uses of Style in Archaeology*, ed. M.W. Conkey and C.A. Hastorf, Cambridge: Cambridge University Press, 1990, pp. 44–51.

Horner, I.B., *The Book of Discipline: Vinaya Pitaka, Vol. II Suttavibhanga*, London: Pali Text Society, 1940; repr. 1982.

Khan, Mohammad Bahadar, M. Habibullah Khan Khattak, Faiz-ur-Rehman and Mohammad Aqleem Khan, *Bhir Mound: The First City of Taxila (Excavation Report 1998–2002)*, Lahore: Government of Pakistan, Department of Archaeology and Museum & National Fund for Cultural Heritage, 2002.

Khare, M.D., 'Pottery from the Excavation', in *Nagarjunakonda (1954–60) volume II (The Historical Period), Memoirs of Archaeological Survey of India*, ed. K.V. Soundara Rajan, no. 75, New Delhi: Archaeological Survey of India, 2006.

Kramer, Carol, 'Ceramic Ethnography', *Annual Review of Anthropology*, vol. 14, 1985, pp. 77–102.

———, *Pottery in Rajasthan: Ethnoarchaeology in Two Indian Cities*, Washington, DC and London: Smithsonian Institution Press, 1997.

Lal, B.B., 'Excavation at Hastinapura and Other Exploration in the Upper Ganga and Sutlej Basin 1950–52', *Ancient India*, vol. 10–11, 1973, pp. 5–151.

Mazumdar, Durgadas, *West Bengal District Gazetteers: Birbhum*, Calcutta: West Bengal District Gazetteers, 1975.

Marshall, John, 'A New Type of Pottery from Baluchistan', *Archaeological Survey of India: Annual Report,* 1904–5, pp. 105–6.

Miller, Daniel, *Artefacts as Categories: A Study of Variability in Central India*, Cambridge: Cambridge University Press, 1985.

Mishra, Anup, *Beyond Pots and Pans: A Study of Chalcolithic Balathal*, Bhopal: Indira Gandhi Rashtriya Manav Sangrahalaya, and New Delhi: Aryan Books International, 2008.

———, 'Time, Tradition and Wheel: Potter's Technology of Central India', in *Past and Present: Ethnoarchaeology in India*, ed. Gautam Sengupta, Suchira Roychoudhury and Sujit Som, New Delhi: Pragati Publication, in collaboration with Centre for Archaeological Studies & Training, Eastern India, Kolkata, 2006.

Narain, A.K. and T.N. Roy, *Excavation at Rajghat (1957–58, 1960–65), Part II: The Pottery*, Varanasi: Banaras Hindu University, 1977.

Nath, Amarendra, *Further Excavations at Pauni, Memoirs of Archaeological Survey of India*, no. 97, New Delhi: Archaeological Survey of India, 1998.

Petrie, W.M. Flinders, *Aims & Methods in Archaeology*, London: MacMillan, 1904.

———, 'British School of Archaeology in Egypt and Egyptian Research Account Twenty-third Year, 1917', *Prehistoric Egypt*, London: British School of Archaeology in Egypt, University College, 1920.

Plogg, Stephen, *New Studies in Archaeology: Stylistic Variation in Prehistoric Ceramics Analysis in the American Southwest*, Cambridge: Cambridge University Press, 1980.

Raman, K.V., *Excavations at Uraiyur (Tiruchurapalli) 1965–69*, Madras: University of Madras, 1988.

Rice, Prudence M., 'Evolution of Specialized Pottery Production: A Trail Model', *Current Anthropology*, vol. 22, no. 3, 1981, pp. 219–40.

Rouse, Irving, 'The Classification of Artifacts in Archaeology', *American Antiquity*, vol. 25, no. 3, 1960, pp. 313–23.

Roux, Vallentine and Daniela Corbetta, *The Potter's Wheel: Craft Specialization and Technical Competence*, New Delhi: Oxford & IBH Publishing Co. Pvt. Ltd, 1989.

Sackett, James R., 'The Meaning of Style in Archaeology: A General Model', *American Antiquity*, vol. 42, 1977, pp. 369–80.

Sankalia, H.D., S.B. Deo, Z.D. Ansari and S. Erhardt, *From History to Prehistory at Nevasa 1954–55*, Poona: Deccan College Post Graduate & Research Institute, 1960.

Sankalia, H.D., B. Subbarao and S.B. Deo, *Excavations at Maheshwar and Navdatoli 1952–53*, Poona: Deccan College Post Graduate & Research Institute, 1958.

Sanyal, Hitesranjan, 'Radher Itihas Prasange Kaekti Katha' (Bengali), *Selected Writings*, Kolkata: Centre for Archaeological Studies & Training, Eastern India (originally published as Occasional Paper No. 32 by Centre for Studies in Social Science in 1980), 2004.

Saraswati, Baidyanath and Nab Kishore Behura, 'Memoir no. 13', *Pottery Techniques in Peasant India*, Calcutta: Anthropological Survey of India, 1966.

Sastri, T.V.G., M. Kasturi Bai and J. Vara Prasad Rao, *Veerapuram, A Type Site for Cultural Study in Krishna Valley*, Hyderbad: Birla Archaeological and Cultural Research Institute, 1984.

Sengupta, Jatindra Chandra, *West Bengal District Gazetteers: Malda*, Calcutta: West Bengal District Gazetteers, 1969.

Sheiffer, M.B. and J.M. Skibo, 'The Explanation of Artifact Variability', *American Antiquity*, no. 62, 1997, pp. 27–55.

Singh, P., *Excavation at Narhan 1988–89*, Varanasi: Banaras Hindu University, 1995.

Sinha, B.P. and B.S. Verma, *Sonpur Excavations 1956 & 1959–62*, Patna: Directorate of Archaeology and Museum, Bihar, 1977.

Sinha, B.P. and Lala Aditya Narain, *Pataliputra Excavation 1955–56*, Patna: Directorate of Archaeology and Museum, Bihar, 1970.

Sinha, B.P. and Sita Ram Roy, *Vaisali Excavation 1958–62*, Patna: Directorate of Archaeology and Museum, Bihar, 1969.

Thomson, W.H., *Census of India 1921, vol. V Bengal, Part II Tables*, Calcutta: Bengal Secretariat Book Depot, 1923.

Vinod, V. and K. Krishnan, 'Potting Skills: An Ethnographic Perspective', *Man and Environment*, vol. XXXVI, no. 1, 2011, pp. 88–91.

Wheeler, R.E.M., 'Arikamedu: An Indo-Roman Trading Station on the East Coast of India', *Ancient India*, no. 2, 1946, pp. 17–124.

Wiessner, Polly, 'Style and Social Information in Kalahari San Projectile Points', *American Antiquity*, vol. 48, no. 2, 1983, pp. 253–75.

Glossary

Bhater handi	rice pot
charan	basin
chhaka khola	sieve for puffed rice
Dab	trough for boiling paddy and feeding cow
Daiyer handi	pot for curd
Debi ghat	ritual pot kept in front of Durga with cocoanut
Dhakni	lid
Dhan chhaka khola	pot for soaking paddy
Dhuki	pot for making pancakes of the Muslim
Dvar ghat	ritual pot in marriage ceremony
handi	cooking pot
handi-kadai	beef pot
Hat	market
Hobishyi handi	pot for cooking ritual food
Hola	offering bowl
Jaler bhand	small pot for water
Jaler dabar	water pot
Kalsi	water pitcher
khapuri/ khuli handi	literally means scull, it draws association in shape pan/roaster
Kodai	frying pan
Kunda handi	worshipped in Durga puja with *darpan* or the mirror
malsa	ritual bowl used for eating food/offering after worship or in period of impurity
Mejla	basin
muri tola	roaster for puffed rice
Pakhir basa	pots serving as bird's nest
Pither khola	bowl for making pan cakes
pujar ghat	worship pot
Rachna handi	ritual pot on offering tray
Raser dabri	pot hung from date tree to receive juice.
Sara	offering tray
Shanti ghat	pot for keeping water of peace
Tal handi	pot for receiving palmyra juice

Tarkarir handi	vegetable making pot
Tawa/chatu	roasting plate
Thala	dish
Tijel	pot with biconic body vegetable frying pot

Technical Glossary

Morphology	form and structure of an object in this case it is pottery
Morphometry	It is the measurement of forms
Multivariate parallel coordinate display	A parallel coordinate display draws an axis for each variable and position them side by side so that they are parallel. The same scale is used for each axis the values for the case are plotted on the axes and connected with a line segment.
Scatterplot Matrix	It plots all possible combination of two or more numeric variables against one another.
Median	the median of a data set has the same number of observations of greater and lesser value.
Lower hinge	it is the first quartile which has 25 per cent observations above and 75 per cent below
Upper hinge	It is the third quartile which has 75 per cent of observations above and 25 per cent below
Box plot	It provides a clear, clean picture of the mid spread, i.e. values between the first and the third quartile of a batch and the outliers.
Distribution curve	A linear graph depicting the distribution of continuous data
Normal distribution	A batch with single peak and symmetrical distribution represented by a bell shaped curve.
Central tendency	It is measured by the mean of the numerical values of a dataset
Kurtosis	the length of the tail of distribution
Platykurtic	the tail of distribution is small
Leptokurtic	the tail of distribution is long
Correlation	It is the relationship between two dependent variables.

For further explanation please refer to any text book on statistics. Archaeologists may find the following books useful:

Shennan, Stephen, *Quantifying Archaeology*, Edinburgh: Edinburgh University Press, 1997 (2nd edn.).

VanPool, Todd L. and Robert D. Leonard, *Quantitative Analysis in Archaeology*, Chichester: Willey-Blackwell, 2011.
Drennan, Robert D., *Statistics for Archaeologists: A Common Sense Approach*, New York: Springer, 2004.

Index